2ND EDITION

Mammals
_of_ Texas
Field Guide

Stan Tekiela

PUBLICATIONS
Adventure
an imprint of AdventureKEEN

To my daughter, Abigail, with all my love

ACKNOWLEDGMENTS

A heartfelt thanks to Rick Bowers, who greatly helped me obtain many of the photos for this book. Special thanks to the National Wildlife Refuge System and the many public and private state and local agencies for stewarding the lands that are critical to the wild mammals we love so much.

Edited by Sandy Livoti and Andrew Mollenkof
Cover and book design by Jonathan Norberg
Silhouettes, tracks, and range maps by Anthony Hertzel

Cover photo: Coyote by Stan Tekiela
See pages 414–415 for photo credits by photographer and page number.

10 9 8 7 6 5 4 3 2 1

Mammals of Texas Field Guide
First Edition 2009
Second Edition 2024
Copyright © 2009 and 2024 by Stan Tekiela
Published by Adventure Publications
An imprint of AdventureKEEN
310 Garfield Street South
Cambridge, Minnesota 55008
(800) 678–7006
www.adventurepublications.net
Printed in China
LCCN 2023028027 (print); 2023028028 (ebook)
ISBN 978-1-64755-425-5 (pbk.); ISBN 978-1-64755-426-2 (ebook)

TABLE OF CONTENTS
Introduction

The Mammals
Mice & Rats

Muskrat

Squirrels

TEXAS MAMMALS

Texas is a great place for wildlife watchers! This state is one of the few places to see magnificent mammals such as Bighorn Sheep and Elk, along with many interesting animals such as the Ringtail and Nine-banded Armadillo. While Northern River Otters play in the lakes and rivers of far eastern Texas, Bobcats thrive in nearly all habitats throughout the state. No matter where you may be in Texas, there is a wide variety of mammals to see and enjoy.

Mammals of Texas Field Guide is an easy-to-use field guide to help the curious nature lover identify all species of mammals found in Texas. It is an all-photographic guide just for Texas, featuring full-color images of animals in their habitats. It is one in a series of unique field guides for Texas that includes birds, mammals, trees, wildflowers, and cacti.

WHAT IS A MAMMAL?

The first mammals appeared in the late Triassic Period, about 200 million years ago. These ancient mammals were small, lacked diversity, and looked nothing like our current-day mammals. During the following Jurassic Period, mammal size and diversity started to increase. Mammals generally started to appear more like today's mammals in the Cenozoic Era, which occurred after the mass extinction of dinosaurs, about 60 million years ago.

Today, modern mammals are a large group of animals that includes nearly 5,500 species around the world, with more than 400 species in North America. Here in Texas we have 157 species, most native to the state. They range from the Least Shrew, a tiny mammal no larger than a human thumb, to the very large and majestic Elk, which can grow to a length of nearly 10 feet (3 m) and weigh up to 1,100 pounds (495 kg). Texas has several large non-native (exotic) animals roaming the state such as the Nilgai and Blackbuck.

All mammals have some common traits or characteristics. Mammals have a backbone (vertebra) and are warm-blooded (endothermic). In endothermic animals, the process of eating and breaking down food in the digestive tract produces heat, which keeps the animal warm even on cold winter nights. Except during periods of hibernation or torpor, the body temperature of mammals stays within a narrow range, just as it does in people. Body temperature is controlled with rapid, open-mouthed breathing known as panting, by shunting blood flow to or away from areas with networks of blood vessels, such as ears, for cooling or conserving heat. When blood flows through vessels that are close to the surface of skin, heat is released and the body cools. When blood flows away from the surface of skin, heat is conserved.

Most mammals are covered with a thick coat of fur or hair. Fur is critical for survival and needs to be kept clean and in good condition. In some animals, such as the Northern River Otter, the fur is so thick it keeps the underlying skin warm and dry even while swimming. Just as birds must preen their feathers to maintain good health, animals spend hours each day licking and "combing" or grooming their fur. You can easily observe this grooming behavior in your pet cat or dog.

Mammals share several other characteristics. All females bear live young and suckle their babies with milk produced from the mammary glands. Mother's milk provides young mammals with total nourishment during the first part of their lives. Also, mammals have sound-conducting bones in their middle ears. These bones give animals the ability to hear as people do and, in many cases, hear much better.

Mammals are diphyodont, meaning they have two sets of teeth. There are milk or deciduous teeth, which fall out, and permanent teeth, also known as adult teeth. Adult teeth usually consist of incisors, canines, premolars, and molars, but these categories can be highly variable in each mammal family. Teeth are often used to classify or group mammals into families in the same manner as the bill of a bird is used to classify or group birds into families.

Reproduction in mammals can be complex and difficult to understand. Many mammals have delayed implantation, which means after the egg and sperm have joined (impregnation), the resulting embryo remains in a suspended state until becoming implanted in the uterine wall. The delay time can be anywhere from a few days to weeks or months. An animal that becomes stressed from lack of food will pass the embryo out of the reproductive tract, and no pregnancy occurs. Conversely, well-fed mothers may have twins or even triplets. Bats and some other species store sperm in the reproductive tract over winter. Impregnation is delayed until spring, and implantation occurs right after impregnation. This process is known as delayed impregnation.

Most mammals are nocturnal, secretive, and don't make a lot of noise, so they tend to go unnoticed. Signs of mammals, such as tracks or scat, are often more commonly seen than the actual animal. However, if you spend some time in the right habitat at the right time of day, your chances of seeing mammals will increase.

IDENTIFICATION STEP-BY-STEP

Fortunately, most large mammals are easy to identify and are not confused with other species. This is not the case, however, with small mammals such as mice or voles. Small animals, while plentiful, can be a challenge to correctly identify because they often have only minor differences in teeth or internal organs and bones.

This field guide is organized by families, starting with small animals, such as shrews and mice, and ending with large mammals such as bear and whale. Within each family section, the animals are in size order from small to large.

Each mammal has four to eight pages of color photos and text, with a silhouette of the animal illustrated on the first description page. Each silhouette is located in a quick-compare tab in the upper right corner. Decide which animal group you are seeing, use the quick-compare tabs to locate the pages for that group, then compare the photos with your animal. If you aren't sure of the identity, the text on description pages explains identifying features that may or may not be easily seen. The first description page for each species also has a compare section with notes about similar species in this field guide. Other pertinent details and the naturalist facts in Stan's Notes will help you correctly identify your mammal in question. Photos of other species will help you identify all of the mammals of Texas.

Thus, every effort has been made to provide relevant identification information including range maps, which can help you eliminate some choices. Colored areas of the maps show where a species can be seen, but not the density of the species. While ranges are accurately depicted, they change on an ongoing basis due to a variety of factors. Please use the maps as intended—as a general guide only.

Finally, if you already know the name of your animal, simply use the index to quickly find the page and learn more about the species from the text and photos.

For many people, an animal's track or silhouette is all they might see of an animal. However, tracks in mud or sand and silhouettes are frequently difficult to identify. Special quick-compare pages, beginning on page 14, are a great place to start the identification process. These pages group similar kinds of animals and tracks side by side for easy comparison. For example, all hoofed animals, such as sheep and bison, are grouped in one section and all dog-like animals are grouped in another. Within the groupings, silhouettes and tracks are illustrated in relative size from small to large. This format allows you to compare one silhouette or track shape and size with another that is similarly shaped and sized. When you don't know whether you're seeing the silhouette or track of a coyote or wolf, a deer or elk, or other similar species, use the quick-compare pages for quick and easy reference.

To begin, find the group that your unknown silhouette or track looks similar to and start comparing. Since each group has relatively few animals, it won't take long to narrow your choices. A ruler can be handy to measure your track and compare it with the size given in the book. To confirm the identity of the silhouette or track and for more detailed information about the animal, refer to the description pages for the number of toes, length of stride, and other distinguishing characteristics.

TAXONOMY OF TEXAS MAMMALS

Biologists classify mammals based on their ancestry and physical characteristics. Texas mammals are grouped into ten scientific orders. Charts with the scientific classification (taxonomy) are shown on the Appendix, pages 392–407. Each of the ten charts starts with one of the orders and shows all scientific families and mammals in that particular order.

CAUTION

Hunting, trapping, possessing and other activities involving animals are regulated by the Texas Parks and Wildlife Department. You should familiarize yourself with the laws and seasons before doing any kill trapping, live trapping, and hunting.

As interesting as all of these animals are, resist any temptation to capture any animal for a pet. Wild animals, even babies, never make good pets. Wild animals often have specific dietary and habitat requirements that rarely can be duplicated in a captive situation, and many will not survive. In many cases, capturing animals for pets is also illegal. This practice not only diminishes the population, it reduces the possibility for future reproduction. Furthermore, some animals are uncommon in Texas, and their populations can be even more quickly depleted.

Live trapping of animals in an attempt to rid your yard of them rarely works. The removal of an animal from its habitat creates a void that is quickly filled with a neighboring animal or its offspring, recreating the original situation. Moreover, an unfortunate animal that is live trapped and moved to a new location often cannot find a habitat with an adequate food supply, shelter, or a territory that is not already occupied. Animals that have been moved often die from exposure to weather, are struck by vehicles while crossing roads, or killed by resident animals. With habitat ranges growing smaller every year, removing just one animal can have a direct impact on the local population of a species. We can all learn to live with our wild animals with just a few modifications to our yards and attitudes. Observe and record animals with your camera, but leave them where they belong—in the wild.

Encounters with wildlife often involve injured or orphaned animals. Many well-intentioned people with little or no resources or knowledge of what is needed try to care for such animals. Injured or orphaned animals deserve the best care, so please do the right thing if you find one and turn it over to a licensed professional wildlife rehabilitator. Information about wildlife rehabilitation in Texas is listed in the resource section of this field guide. The rehabilitation staff may often be able to give you updates on the condition of an animal you bring in and even when it is released. When you take an animal to a rehab center, you might also want to consider making a monetary donation to help cover the costs involved for its care.

Enjoy the Wild Mammals!

Stan

Body length measurements do not include tail.

Average size of the smallest and largest of this group compared to an 8" hand.

Silhouettes are in proportion by average body length. Tracks are in proportion by average largest foot. Front track is on the left and hind is on the right.

Least Shrew
pg. 45
1⁷⁄₈"
1⁄8"   3⁄8"

Desert Shrew
pg. 49
2¼"
¼"   3⁄8"

Eastern Harvest Mouse
pg. 59
2½"
1⁄8"   ½"

Fulvous Harvest Mouse
pg. 55
2¾"
3⁄8"   7⁄8"

Plains Pocket Mouse
pg. 71
3½"
¼"   5⁄8"

Western Harvest Mouse
pg. 59
3½"
¼"   5⁄8"

Southern Short-tailed Shrew pg. 49
3½"
5⁄8"   ½"

Golden Mouse
pg. 65
3¾"
½"   ¾"

Mearns' Grasshopper Mouse pg. 75
3¾"
½"   7⁄8"

Cactus Mouse
pg. 64
3¾"
½"   1"

14

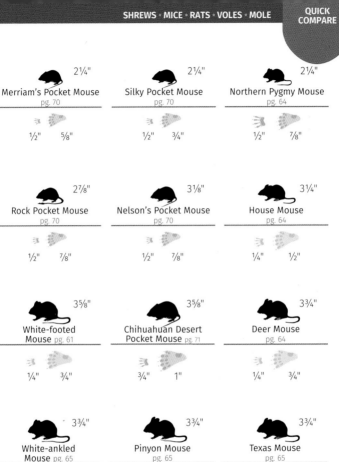

2¼"
Merriam's Pocket Mouse
pg. 70

½" ⅝"

2¼"
Silky Pocket Mouse
pg. 70

½" ¾"

2¼"
Northern Pygmy Mouse
pg. 64

½" ⅞"

2⅞"
Rock Pocket Mouse
pg. 70

½" ⅞"

3⅛"
Nelson's Pocket Mouse
pg. 70

½" ⅞"

3¼"
House Mouse
pg. 64

¼" ½"

3⅝"
White-footed Mouse pg. 61

¼" ¾"

3⅝"
Chihuahuan Desert Pocket Mouse pg. 71

¾" 1"

3¾"
Deer Mouse
pg. 64

¼" ¾"

3¾"
White-ankled Mouse pg. 65

⅝" ⅞"

3¾"
Pinyon Mouse
pg. 65

¾" 1"

3¾"
Texas Mouse
pg. 65

¾" 1"

Similar species on next page

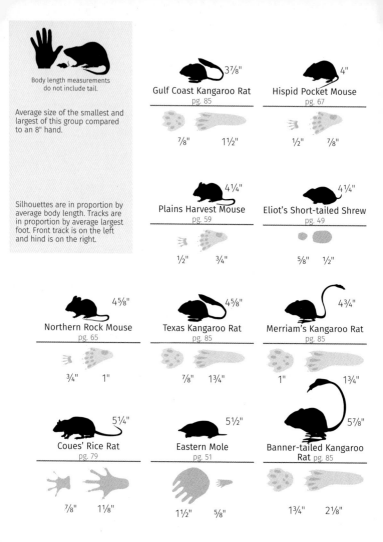

Body length measurements do not include tail.

Average size of the smallest and largest of this group compared to an 8" hand.

Silhouettes are in proportion by average body length. Tracks are in proportion by average largest foot. Front track is on the left and hind is on the right.

3⅞"

Gulf Coast Kangaroo Rat
pg. 85

⅞" 1½"

4"

Hispid Pocket Mouse
pg. 67

½" ⅞"

4¼"

Plains Harvest Mouse
pg. 59

½" ¾"

4¼"

Eliot's Short-tailed Shrew
pg. 49

⅝" ½"

4⅝"

Northern Rock Mouse
pg. 65

¾" 1"

4⅝"

Texas Kangaroo Rat
pg. 85

⅞" 1¾"

4¾"

Merriam's Kangaroo Rat
pg. 85

1" 1¾"

5¼"

Coues' Rice Rat
pg. 79

⅞" 1⅛"

5½"

Eastern Mole
pg. 51

1½" ⅝"

5⅞"

Banner-tailed Kangaroo Rat pg. 85

1¾" 2⅛"

Northern Grasshopper
Mouse pg. 73

4"

1/2"   1"

Cotton Mouse
pg. 65

4"

3/4"   1"

Woodland Vole
pg. 103

4 1/8"

1/4"   5/8"

Mexican Spiny Pocket
Mouse pg. 71

4 1/4"

3/4"   1 1/4"

Prairie Vole
pg. 107

4 1/2"

1/2"   7/8"

Mexican Vole
pg. 107

4 5/8"

1/2"   3/4"

Brush Mouse
pg. 65

4 7/8"

3/4"   1"

Marsh Rice Rat
pg. 77

5"

1/2"   1"

Ord's Kangaroo Rat
pg. 81

5"

1 1/4"   1 3/4"

Yellow-nosed
Cotton Rat pg. 91

6 3/4"

3/4"   1"

Tawny-bellied
Cotton Rat pg. 91

6 3/4"

3/4"   1"

Black Rat
pg. 101

6 7/8"

1"   1 3/8"

Similar species on next page **17**

Body length measurements
do not include tail.

Average size of the smallest and
largest of this group compared
to an 8" hand.

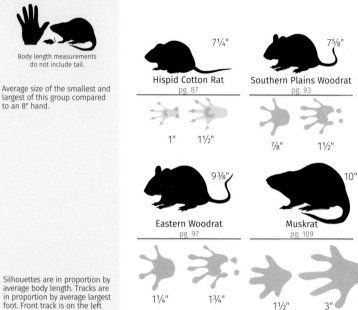

Hispid Cotton Rat
pg. 87
7¼"
1"   1½"

Southern Plains Woodrat
pg. 93
7⅝"
⅞"   1½"

Eastern Woodrat
pg. 97
9⅜"
1¼"   1¾"

Muskrat
pg. 109
10"
1½"   3"

Silhouettes are in proportion by
average body length. Tracks are
in proportion by average largest
foot. Front track is on the left
and hind is on the right.

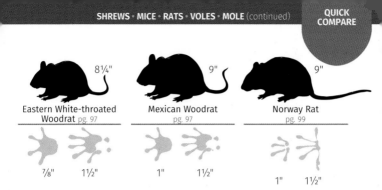

Eastern White-throated
Woodrat pg. 97
8¼"
⅞"   1½"

Mexican Woodrat
pg. 97
9"
1"   1½"

Norway Rat
pg. 99
9"
1"   1½"

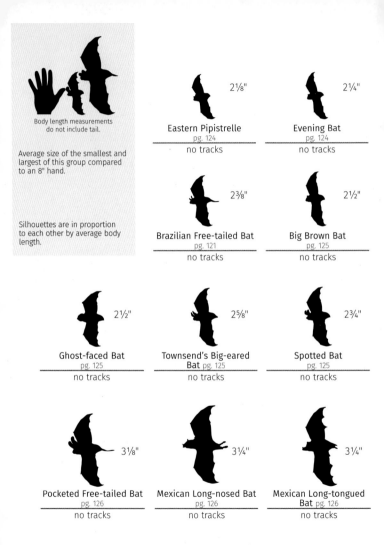

Body length measurements
do not include tail.

Average size of the smallest and
largest of this group compared
to an 8" hand.

Silhouettes are in proportion
to each other by average body
length.

2⅛"

Eastern Pipistrelle
pg. 124
no tracks

2¼"

Evening Bat
pg. 124
no tracks

2⅜"

Brazilian Free-tailed Bat
pg. 121
no tracks

2½"

Big Brown Bat
pg. 125
no tracks

2½"

Ghost-faced Bat
pg. 125
no tracks

2⅝"

**Townsend's Big-eared
Bat** pg. 125
no tracks

2¾"

Spotted Bat
pg. 125
no tracks

3⅛"

Pocketed Free-tailed Bat
pg. 126
no tracks

3¼"

Mexican Long-nosed Bat
pg. 126
no tracks

3¼"

**Mexican Long-tongued
Bat** pg. 126
no tracks

Western Small-footed Myotis pg. 124 — 2¼"
no tracks

Fringed Myotis pg. 125 — 2⅜"
no tracks

Western Pipistrelle pg. 125 — 2⅜"
no tracks

Silver-haired Bat pg. 125 — 2½"
no tracks

Eastern Red Bat pg. 125 — 2½"
no tracks

California Myotis pg. 125 — 2½"
no tracks

Yuma Myotis pg. 125 — 2¾"
no tracks

Hoary Bat pg. 125 — 3"
no tracks

Hairy-legged Vampire Bat pg. 125 — 3"
no tracks

Long-legged Myotis pg. 126 — 3¼"
no tracks

Western Red Bat pg. 126 — 3½"
no tracks

Southeastern Myotis pg. 126 — 3½"
no tracks

Similar species on next page **21**

Body length measurements
do not include tail.

Average size of the smallest and
largest of this group compared
to an 8" hand.

Cave Myotis
pg. 126
no tracks
3¾"

Pallid Bat
pg. 126
no tracks
3⅞"

Seminole Bat
pg. 126
no tracks
4⅜"

Southern Yellow Bat
pg. 127
no tracks
4⅝"

Silhouettes are in proportion
to each other by average body
length.

22

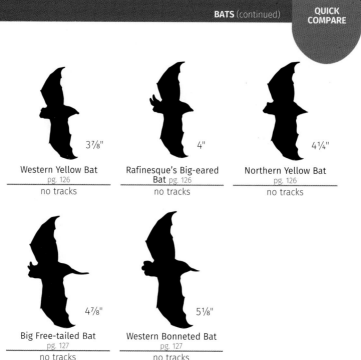

Western Yellow Bat
pg. 126
3⅞"
no tracks

Rafinesque's Big-eared Bat pg. 126
4"
no tracks

Northern Yellow Bat
pg. 126
4¼"
no tracks

Big Free-tailed Bat
pg. 127
4⅞"
no tracks

Western Bonneted Bat
pg. 127
5⅛"
no tracks

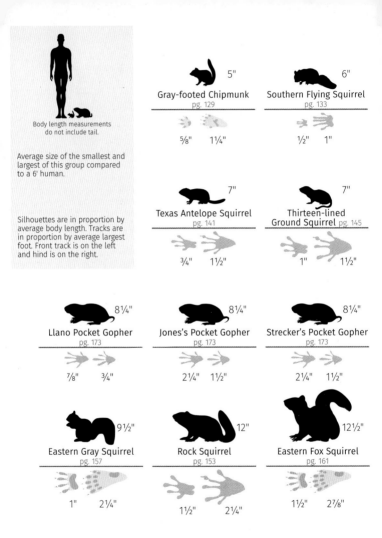

Body length measurements do not include tail.

Average size of the smallest and largest of this group compared to a 6' human.

Silhouettes are in proportion by average body length. Tracks are in proportion by average largest foot. Front track is on the left and hind is on the right.

Gray-footed Chipmunk
pg. 129
5"
5/8"   1 1/4"

Southern Flying Squirrel
pg. 133
6"
1/2"   1"

Texas Antelope Squirrel
pg. 141
7"
3/4"   1 1/2"

Thirteen-lined
Ground Squirrel pg. 145
7"
1"   1 1/2"

Llano Pocket Gopher
pg. 173
8 1/4"
7/8"   3/4"

Jones's Pocket Gopher
pg. 173
8 1/4"
2 1/4"   1 1/2"

Strecker's Pocket Gopher
pg. 173
8 1/4"
2 1/4"   1 1/2"

Eastern Gray Squirrel
pg. 157
9 1/2"
1"   2 1/4"

Rock Squirrel
pg. 153
12"
1 1/2"   2 1/4"

Eastern Fox Squirrel
pg. 161
12 1/2"
1 1/2"   2 7/8"

24

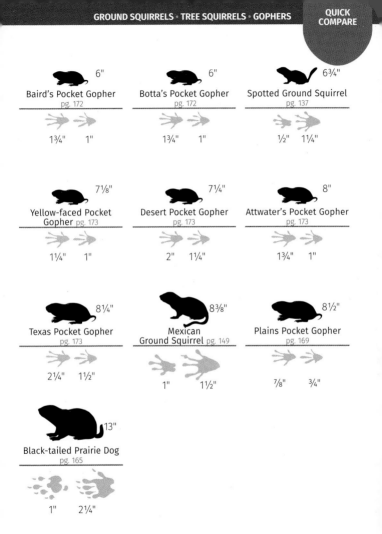

6"
Baird's Pocket Gopher
pg. 172

1¾"   1"

6"
Botta's Pocket Gopher
pg. 172

1¾"   1"

6¾"
Spotted Ground Squirrel
pg. 137

½"   1¼"

7⅛"
Yellow-faced Pocket Gopher pg. 173

1¼"   1"

7¼"
Desert Pocket Gopher
pg. 173

2"   1¼"

8"
Attwater's Pocket Gopher
pg. 173

1¾"   1"

8¼"
Texas Pocket Gopher
pg. 173

2¼"   1½"

8⅜"
**Mexican
Ground Squirrel** pg. 149

1"   1½"

8½"
Plains Pocket Gopher
pg. 169

⅞"   ¾"

13"
Black-tailed Prairie Dog
pg. 165

1"   2¼"

Body length measurements do not include tail.

Average size of the smallest and largest of this group compared to a 6' human.

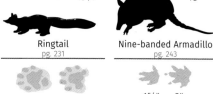

13¾"
Ringtail
pg. 231

1¾"   2⅝"

18"
Nine-banded Armadillo
pg. 243

1⅝"   2"

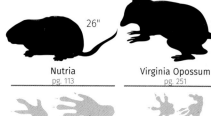

26"
Nutria
pg. 113

2½"   5"

27½"
Virginia Opossum
pg. 251

1½"   2"

Silhouettes are in proportion by average body length. Tracks are in proportion by average largest foot. Front track is on the left and hind is on the right.

23"

North American
Porcupine pg. 247

2¼"   3¼"

24½"

Northern Raccoon
pg. 235

2¾"   4"

27½"

White-nosed Coati
pg. 239

2¼"   3¼"

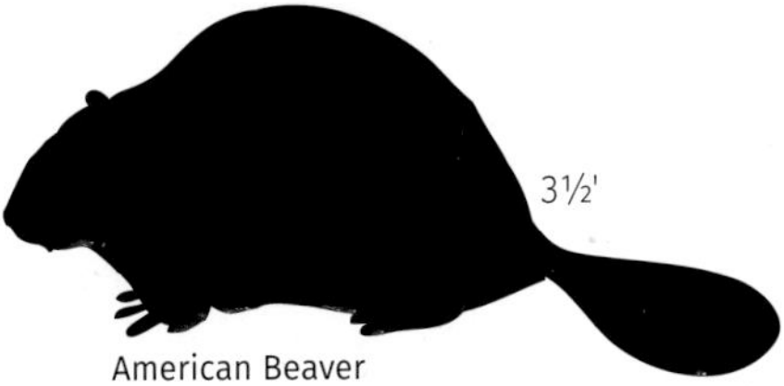

3½'

American Beaver
pg. 117

3"   5"

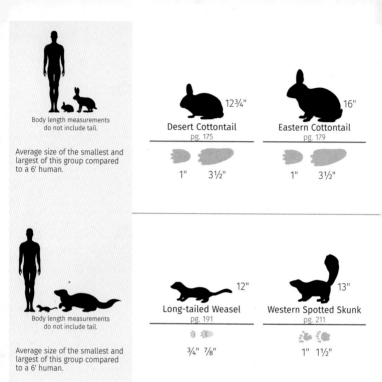

Body length measurements
do not include tail.

Average size of the smallest and
largest of this group compared
to a 6' human.

Desert Cottontail
pg. 175
12¾"

1"   3½"

Eastern Cottontail
pg. 179
16"

1"   3½"

Body length measurements
do not include tail.

Average size of the smallest and
largest of this group compared
to a 6' human.

Long-tailed Weasel
pg. 191
12"

¾"   ⅞"

Western Spotted Skunk
pg. 211
13"

1"   1½"

Mink
pg. 195
17"

1½"   2⅝"

Black-footed Ferret
pg. 199
17¼"

2¼"   2⅜"

Silhouettes are in proportion by
average body length. Tracks are
in proportion by average largest
foot. Front track is on the left
and hind is on the right.

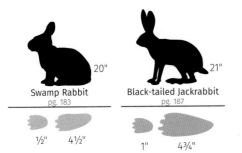

Swamp Rabbit
pg. 183
20"
½" 4½"

Black-tailed Jackrabbit
pg. 187
21"
1" 4¾"

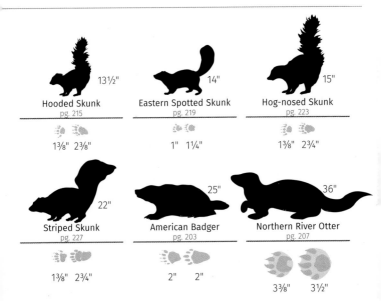

Hooded Skunk
pg. 215
13½"
1⅜" 2⅜"

Eastern Spotted Skunk
pg. 219
14"
1" 1¼"

Hog-nosed Skunk
pg. 223
15"
1⅜" 2¾"

Striped Skunk
pg. 227
22"
1⅜" 2¾"

American Badger
pg. 203
25"
2" 2"

Northern River Otter
pg. 207
36"
3⅜" 3½"

29

Body length measurements
do not include tail.

Average size of the smallest and
largest of this group compared
to a 6' human.

Silhouettes are in proportion by
average body length. Tracks are
in proportion by average largest
foot. Front track is on the left
and hind is on the right.

18"

Kit Fox
pg. 255

1½" 1⅜"

18"

Swift Fox
pg. 259

1½" 1⅜"

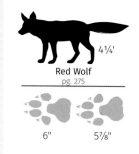

4¼'

Red Wolf
pg. 275

6" 5⅞"

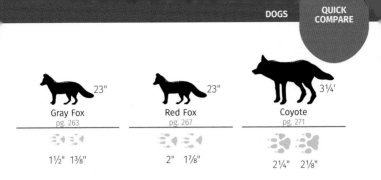

Gray Fox
pg. 263

1½" 1⅜"

Red Fox
pg. 267

2"   1⅞"

Coyote
pg. 271

2¼"   2⅛"

23"   23"   3¼'

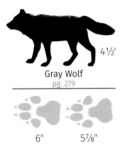

Gray Wolf
pg. 279

6"   5⅞"

4½'

Body length measurements
do not include tail.

Average size of the smallest and
largest of this group compared
to a 6' human.

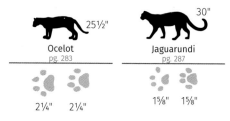

Ocelot
pg. 283

25½"

2¼"   2¼"

Jaguarundi
pg. 287

30"

1⅝"   1⅝"

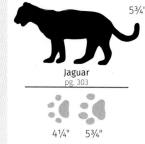

Jaguar
pg. 303

5¾'

4¼"   5¾"

Silhouettes are in proportion by
average body length. Tracks are
in proportion by average largest
foot. Front track is on the left
and hind is on the right.

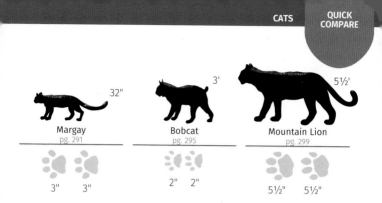

32"

Margay
pg. 291

3"   3"

3'

Bobcat
pg. 295

2"   2"

5½'

Mountain Lion
pg. 299

5½"   5½"

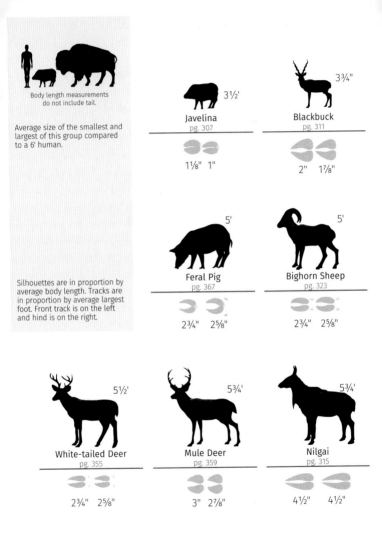

Body length measurements
do not include tail.

Average size of the smallest and
largest of this group compared
to a 6' human.

Silhouettes are in proportion by
average body length. Tracks are
in proportion by average largest
foot. Front track is on the left
and hind is on the right.

Javelina
pg. 307

3½'

1⅛"   1"

Blackbuck
pg. 311

3¾"

2"   1⅞"

Feral Pig
pg. 367

5'

2¾"   2⅝"

Bighorn Sheep
pg. 323

5'

2¾"   2⅝"

White-tailed Deer
pg. 355

5½'

2¾"   2⅝"

Mule Deer
pg. 359

5¾'

3"   2⅞"

Nilgai
pg. 315

5¾'

4½"   4½"

4¼'

Pronghorn
pg. 331

3"   2⅞"

4½'

Barbary Sheep
pg. 319

2¼"   2⅛"

4½'

Burro
pg. 335

2½"   2½"

5'

Fallow Deer
pg. 343

3"   2⅞"

5¼'

Sika Deer
pg. 347

2¼"   2⅛"

5½'

Axis Deer
pg. 351

2½"   2⅜"

5'

Feral Horse
pg. 339

4"   4"

8¼'

Elk
pg. 363

4¼"   4⅛"

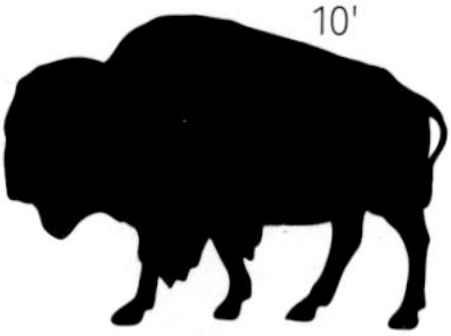

10'

Bison
pg. 327

6½"   6⅜"

35

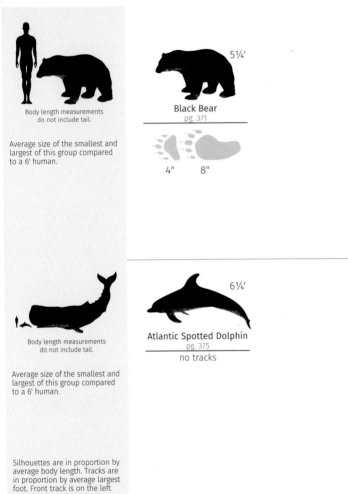

Body length measurements
do not include tail.

Average size of the smallest and
largest of this group compared
to a 6' human.

Black Bear
pg. 371

5¼'

4"   8"

Body length measurements
do not include tail.

Average size of the smallest and
largest of this group compared
to a 6' human.

Atlantic Spotted Dolphin
pg. 375
no tracks

6¼'

Silhouettes are in proportion by
average body length. Tracks are
in proportion by average largest
foot. Front track is on the left
and hind is on the right.

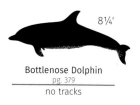

8¼'

Bottlenose Dolphin
pg. 379
no tracks

Body length measurements
do not include tail.

Average size of the smallest and
largest of this group compared
to a 6' human.

Silhouettes are in proportion by
average body length. Tracks are
in proportion by average largest
foot. Front track is on the left
and hind is on the right.

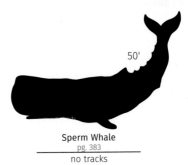

50'

Sperm Whale
pg. 383

no tracks

Common Name
Scientific name

FORMER
RANGE

Family: common family name (scientific family name)

Size: (L) average length or range of length of body from head to rump; for marine (M) male and (F) female, from head to tail; (T) average length or range of length of tail; (H) average height or range of height to top of back

Weight: average weight or range of weight; may include (M) male and (F) female weights

Description: brief description of the mammal; may include color morphs, seasonal variations or differences between male and female

Origin/Age: native or non-native to Texas or the Gulf waters off the coast; average life span in the wild

Compare: notes about other species that look similar and the pages on which they can be found; may include extra information to help identify

Habitat: environment (e.g., deserts, scrublands, grasslands, canyons, fields, forests); may include elevations

Home: description of nest, burrow or den; may include other related information

Food: herbivore, carnivore, insectivore, omnivore or ichthyophagous; what the animal eats most of the time; may include other related information

Sounds: vocalization or other noises the animal creates; may include variant sounds or other information

Breeding: mating season; length of gestation

Young: number of offspring born per year and when; may include description or birth weight

summer coat

winter coat

silver morph   dark morph

scat

Signs: evidence that the animal was there or is near; may include a description of scat; other comments

Activity: diurnal, nocturnal, crepuscular; other comments

Tracks: forepaw and hind paw or hoof size and shape, largest size first; pattern of tracks; description of prints, which may include tail drag mark or stride; other comments

Tracks and Pattern

Stan's Notes: Interesting gee-whiz natural history information. This can be something to look or listen for, or something to help positively identify the animal such as remarkable features. May include additional photos to illustrate juveniles, nests, unique behaviors, and other key characteristics.

den entrance

sample page

kits

Similar species on next page in some cases

Least Shrew
Cryptotis parva

Family: Shrews (Soricidae)

Size: L 1½–2¼" (4–5.5 cm); T ½–¾" (1–2 cm)

Weight: ¼ oz. (7 g)

Description: Mostly brown above, but fur can be gray. Lighter belly. Pointed snout. Tiny dark eyes. Short tail, never more than twice as long as the hind foot. Small pink feet. Ears barely visible.

Origin/Age: native; 1–2 years

Compare: Slightly smaller than the Desert Shrew (pg. 49), which has a longer tail and occurs in the arid western half of Texas. Smaller than the Southern Short-tailed Shrew (pg. 49), which has a tail about the same length, but a larger body and is darker overall.

Habitat: fields, grasslands, meadows, shrubby areas

Home: chamber in an underground burrow, nest made with dried leaves and grasses

Food: insectivore, carnivore; beetles, crickets, spiders, grasshoppers, slugs, earthworms, snails, small mammals

Sounds: inconsequential; sharp squeaks and high-pitched whistles can be heard from a distance up to 2 feet (61 cm)

Breeding: Mar–Nov mating; 21–23 days gestation

Young: 1–6 offspring several times per year; born naked with eyes closed, weaned at about 3 weeks

Signs: partially eaten insects near the burrow entrance; extremely tiny, dark scat, widely scattered

Activity: nocturnal, diurnal; may be more active during the day in summer, when nights are shorter

Tracks: hind paw ¼–½" (0.6–1 cm) long, forepaw slightly smaller; 1 set of 4 tracks, but prints are so close together they appear as 1 track; 4 prints together are 1 square inch (6.4 sq. cm), often lacks a tail drag mark due to its short tail

Least Shrew (continued)

Stan's Notes: One of Texas's smallest and least studied shrew species, thus not much is known about its biology. Range in the United States is widespread from Minnesota to Texas to Florida and up the entire East coast, excluding New England.

Sometimes called Bee Shrew because it supposedly lives in beehives; however, this has never been studied or widely reported and may be a reference to the animal's small size. It has been reported to take up residency in a beehive while eating the bees that occupy it.

Hunts for invertebrates by probing through leaf litter with its nose, smelling for prey. Often feeds only on the internal organs of large insects. Subdues prey by capturing and biting off the head, which makes it easier to get to internal organs. Like other shrews, it eats nearly its own body weight in food each day. When food is abundant it will cache some for later consumption.

While most other shrew species are solitary, the Least Shrew is apparently more social, with many individuals in one nest. It is thought that owls, particularly Barn Owls, are the major predators of the Least Shrew. In one study, Least Shrews made up 41 percent of the diet of one Barn Owl pair. In another pair, Least Shrews made up 73 percent of the diet.

Similar species on next page **47**

Shrews are small mammals that look similar to mice, but shrews have longer, more pointed snouts, tiny well-concealed ears and well-haired tails that are rather short. Fur color ranges from gray to brown or black.

All shrew species in Texas eat insects and other small animals such as voles and moles. With extremely high metabolic rates, they forage for food round-the-clock, consuming their body weight in food every 24 hours. Shrews are the only known mammal to have a toxic saliva, which presumably helps to subdue prey. They do not have a way to inject the saliva into prey so it must be "chewed" in—not a very efficient procedure.

While all shrews have poor eyesight, they have an excellent sense of smell and the ability to hear in very high frequencies. Some are thought to be able to sense electromagnetic fields, enabling them to locate prey in complete darkness.

They live in the shallow tunnels of other small mammals, such as voles, or dig their own burrows. Some nests are beneath fallen logs and other debris.

Desert Shrew 2–2½"

Southern Short-tailed Shrew 3–4"

Elliot's Short-tailed Shrew 4–4½"

Eastern Mole
Scalopus aquaticus

Family: Moles (Talpidae)

Size: L 4–7" (10–18 cm); T ¾–1¼" (2–3 cm)

Weight: 3–5 oz. (85–142 g)

Description: Short silky fur, dark brown to gray with a silver sheen. Long pointed snout. Very large, naked front feet, more wide than long and resembling human hands with palms turned outward. Very short, nearly naked tail. Pinpoint eyes, frequently hidden by fur. Male slightly larger than female.

Origin/Age: native; 1–2 years

Compare: Very unique-looking animal with extremely short legs and large, human-like pink hands for paws. No eyes and a short tail. Smaller than the Plains Pocket Gopher (pg. 169), which has eyes and a longer tail.

Habitat: dry grassy areas, fields, lawns, gardens, loose well-drained soils

Home: burrow, tunnels usually are 4–20" (10–50 cm) underground in summer, deeper tunnels below the frost line during winter, nest is in a chamber connected to a tunnel, with separate chambers for giving birth and raising young

Food: insectivore, herbivore; insects, grubs, roots, worms

Sounds: inconsequential; rarely, if ever, heard

Breeding: Feb–Mar mating; 32–42 days gestation

Young: 2–6 offspring once per year in early spring; born naked with eyes closed, weaned at 30–40 days, leaves nest chamber when weaned

tail

Signs: ridges of soil from tunnel construction just below the surface of the ground, sometimes small piles of soil on the ground (molehills) from digging deeper permanent tunnels

Activity: diurnal, nocturnal; active year-round, does not appear to time its activities with the rising and setting of the sun

Tracks: hind paw ⅝" (1.5 cm) long with 5 toes, forepaw 1½" (4 cm) long with 5 toes; individual tracks are indistinguishable and create a single groove with claw marks, sometimes has a tail drag mark; spends almost all of its time in its underground tunnel system, so tracks are rarely seen

52

Stan's Notes: The first time this animal was described in records was when a drowned mole was found in a well. It was presumed, in error, to be aquatic; hence the Latin species name *aquaticus*, which also refers to the slight webbing between its toes. This is the most subterranean mammal in Texas, spending 99 percent of its life underground. Also called Common Mole or just Mole.

The Eastern Mole has no external ears. Its tiny eyes are covered with skin and detect light only, not shapes or colors. It has large white teeth, unlike the shrews, which have chestnut or tan teeth. Uses its very sensitive, flexible snout to find food by smelling and sensing vibrations with its whiskers. The nap of its short fur can lie forward or backward, making it easier to travel in either direction in tight tunnels. A narrow pelvis allows it to somersault often and reverse its heading.

Excavates its own tunnel system. Uses its front feet to dig while pushing loosened soil back and out of the way with its hind feet. Able to dig 12 inches (30 cm) per minute in loose soil. Digging and tunneling is beneficial to the environment; it aerates the soil and allows moisture to penetrate deeper into the ground.

Searches for subterranean insects, earthworms, some plant roots, and other food in temporary tunnels, usually located just below the surface of the ground. Deeper permanent tunnels are used for living, nesting, and depositing waste. Will move to even deeper tunnels below the frost line during winter.

The male will seek out a female in her tunnel to mate during late winter. It is thought that a female rarely leaves her tunnel system except when a young female leaves the tunnels of her mother to establish her own.

Unlike most other small mammals, it reproduces only once each year. Not preyed upon as heavily due to its burrowing (fossorial) life, so does not need to reproduce often.

Fulvous Harvest Mouse
Reithrodontomys fulvescens

Family: Rats and Mice (Muridae)

Size: L 2½–3" (6–7.5 cm); T 3¼–4" (8–10 cm)

Weight: ½–1 oz. (14–28 g)

Description: Overall golden tan to rust, peppered with black. Orange line along each side dividing the rusty body and a white underbelly. Large ears, covered with rusty hairs. White-to-gray belly. Large eyes. Tail is longer than the head and body combined, only slightly bicolored, not tufted.

Origin/Age: native; 1–2 years

Compare: Smaller than Plains Harvest Mouse (pg. 59), which has a distinctly bicolored tail that is less than half the length of its head and body. Smaller than Western Harvest Mouse (pg. 59), which has a tail equal to the head and body length.

Habitat: dry grassy areas, fields, roadsides, shrubby areas, desert scrub, wetlands

Home: underground burrow with multiple chambers, aboveground ball-shaped nest made of dried grass, 5–6" (13–15 cm) diameter, occasionally low in a shrub or small tree or attached to grass stems, often in an old bird nest

Food: herbivore, insectivore; seeds, vegetation, fruit, fresh green shoots in spring, insects

Sounds: inconsequential; high-pitched trilling call

Breeding: early Feb–Oct mating; 21–23 days gestation

Young: 2–6 (average 3) pups up to 4 times per year; born naked with eyes closed, weighing about ½ oz. (14 g)

grooved incisor

Signs: surface runways, ball-shaped nest made of dried grass on the ground, most obvious after a field or grassland fire, nest is sometimes attached to grass stems or in a small tree or shrub

Activity: mostly nocturnal; active year-round, often huddles in nest during the day with other members of its family

Tracks: hind paw ⅞" (2.3 cm) long with 5 toes, forepaw ⅜" (0.9 cm) long with 4 toes; sometimes has a tail drag mark

Stan's Notes: One of the smallest of harvest mice, ranging from Alabama west to central Texas and parts of the Trans-Pecos. It harvests dried grass to build a large softball-sized nest, hence the common name. Known to use the nest of a bird as a base to build a ball nest of dried grass. Mainly uses underground burrows, but may use more than one nest in its home range including 1–2 in shrubs. Uses the runways and burrows of other animals such as pocket gophers and voles.

Considered to be a good mouse to have around because it feeds heavily on weed seeds. Stores many seeds in underground caches. A big climber, jumping into trees and shrubs and scurrying about among the branches. Non-territorial and tolerant of one another. Rarely enters homes or other buildings.

A female usually has up to four litters per season. However, it has been reported that a captive female harvest mouse reproduced as many as 14 times, giving birth to a total of 58 young.

The Fulvous and other harvest mice species have been classified in *Reithrodontomys*, a genus separate from other small mice. One way to identify a harvest mouse is by the groove front-and-center in its upper incisor teeth, which other small mice lack. In addition, the harvest mouse lacks the fur-lined cheek pouches of pocket mice. Although some pocket mice species have grooved incisors like those of harvest mice, this is not a feature that a casual observer will see.

Similar species on next page **57**

Harvest mice are a group of small mice that look like miniature Deer Mice (pg. 64) with long narrow tails. All are found in grassy areas, feed on grass seeds, build softball-sized nests of dried plant material, and live aboveground and belowground.

There are five harvest mouse species in the United States, with four occurring in Texas. The Eastern Harvest Mouse lives in the far eastern quarter of the state. Its tail length is equal to the length of its head and body. The Western Harvest Mouse occurs along the far western edge and in the panhandle of Texas and also has a tail length equal to its head and body. Plains Harvest Mouse occupies the western two-thirds of the state and has a tail that is shorter than the length of its head and body combined.

Eastern Harvest Mouse 2¼–2¾"

Western Harvest Mouse 3–4"

Plains Harvest Mouse 4–4½"

White-footed Mouse
Peromyscus leucopus

Family: Rats and Mice (Muridae)

Size: L 3–4¼" (7.5–10.5 cm); T 2–3½" (5–9 cm)

Weight: ⅜–1¼ oz. (11–35 g)

Description: Reddish brown back and sides with white chest, belly, legs and feet. Tail is brown above, white below and shorter than the head and body. Large bulging eyes. Large, round naked ears.

Origin/Age: native; 1–2 years

Compare: Hard to distinguish from Deer Mouse (pg. 64). White-footed Mouse is usually slightly smaller, with smaller ears and a slightly shorter tail.

Habitat: wide variety such as woodlands, fields, around dwellings, river bottoms

Home: nest, loose round mass of plant material with a hollow center, lined with animal hair, milkweed silk, or other soft material, usually underneath a log or other shelter or inside a log or standing tree; abandons nest when completely soiled with urine and builds another

Food: omnivore; seeds, vegetation, fruit, nuts, insects, baby birds, carrion

Sounds: inconsequential; scratching or scampering can be heard, drums front feet on ground if threatened

Breeding: year-round, but mainly Mar–Oct mating; 22–23 days gestation

Young: 4–6 pups up to 3–4 times per year; born with eyes and ears closed, all gray when very young, dull brown after 40–50 days, reddish brown in a couple months

Signs: stockpiles of seeds near nest, strong smell of urine in the areas it often visits; small, hard black scat the size of a pinhead

Activity: nocturnal in summer, more diurnal in winter; remains in the nest during the coldest winter days

Tracks: hind paw ¾" (2 cm) long with 5 toes, forepaw ¼" (0.6 cm) long with 4 toes; 1 set of 4 tracks; sometimes has a tail drag mark

Stan's Notes: A common small mammal, found in a variety of habitats. Generally more territorial and aggressive than the mild-mannered Deer Mouse (pg. 64). Will bite if handled. Like other mice, it is an important part of the ecosystem, being prey for many animals such as foxes, coyotes, hawks, owls, and more.

Its range extends from the East coast to Montana and down through Texas to southern Mexico. The White-footed is a great swimmer that has dispersed to islands in the largest lakes.

An excellent climber, often climbing trees to find seeds. Uses its tail to help maintain balance when climbing. Enjoys a variety of food, but eats mainly seeds. Caches food in fall, often nearby in an empty bird nest. Some caches contain over a quart of seeds from a variety of plants. Enters homes in fall for shelter and food.

pup

In the coldest winter months it enters a condition resembling hibernation (torpor), in which body temperature drops and rate of breathing slows from 700 breaths per minute to as few as 60.

Young leave the nest after only 2 weeks and start to breed at about 40 days. They rarely live more than a year, with entirely new populations produced annually. A carrier (vector) for ticks that carry Lyme disease. Use care when cleaning out old mouse nests. Avoid breathing in any airborne dust or particles when removing old nests.

Additional Mouse Species

To many people, all mice look the same. There are many common features among species that make differentiation very difficult. To make things worse, some species hybridize, creating varieties that defy identification. While some species, such as the House Mouse, can be best identified by where they are found, firm identification of mice should be left to the experts. Deer Mouse is found in all counties. Golden Mouse is only in the far eastern corner of Texas. Pinyon Mouse occurs in just a few counties near the panhandle. Texas Mouse is seen in central and northern parts of the state. Northern Rock Mouse is found only in the Trans-Pecos region.

Northern Pygmy Mouse 2–2½"

House Mouse 2½–4"

Deer Mouse 3–4½"

Cactus Mouse 3–4½"

Golden Mouse 3½–4"

White-ankled Mouse 3½–4"

Pinyon Mouse 3½–4"

Texas Mouse 3½–4"

Cotton Mouse 3¾–4¼"

Northern Rock Mouse 4–5¼"

Brush Mouse 4¼–5½"

Hispid Pocket Mouse
Chaetodipus hispidus

Family: Kangaroo Rats and Pocket Mice (Heteromyidae)

Size: L 3¾–4½" (9.5–10.5 cm); T 3–3½" (7.5–9 cm)

Weight: 1½ oz. (43 g)

Description: Overall orange to yellowish brown with a wash of black hairs concentrated near the center of the back and rump, giving a grizzled look. Often a thin, pale orange line on the sides from cheek to near the base of tail. White-to-cream chest, belly, legs, and feet. Large hind foot with a naked sole. Tail is slightly shorter than the body, bicolored, dark above, tan below, well haired and lacking a tuft. Large eyes. Small round ears with dark tips.

Origin/Age: native; 1–3 years

Compare: Much larger than the tiny Silky Pocket Mouse (pg. 70). Merriam's Pocket Mouse (pg. 70) is also smaller and has white spots by its ears.

Habitat: sagebrush, dry rocky habitats, sandy soils, grassy areas along fences (fencerows), ditches

Home: nest made of dried plant material, in an underground burrow with vertical entrance holes, 1" (2.5 cm) wide, 1 hole surrounded by a dirt pile

Food: herbivore, insectivore; mainly seeds, also fruit, nuts, insects, earthworms

Sounds: inconsequential; scratching or scampering can be heard

Breeding: Apr–Aug mating; 20–23 days gestation

Young: 3–8 (average 6) pups up to 2 times per year; born naked and deaf with eyes closed

cheek pocket

naked sole

Signs: evidence of a burrow under clumps of vegetation, runways and surface tunnels radiating from the entrance of burrow, some entrances have dirt piled up; scat not seen

Activity: nocturnal; remains in the nest during the coldest winter days or during heavy rain in summer

Tracks: hind paw ⅞" (2.3 cm) long with 5 toes, forepaw ½" (1 cm) long with 4 toes; 1 set of 4 tracks along trails leading to and from the burrow

Stan's Notes: The common name "Hispid," Latin for "stiff hairs," describes the scattering of longer dark hairs on the body of this mouse. The naked soles on its hind feet also help to identify it.

The most widespread and common pocket mouse in Texas, it is common along roads and fence lines. Almost always found in areas with sandy soils and only scattered plant growth. Usually avoids dense stands of grass or other vegetation.

Digs its own burrow with unique entrance holes that appear like auger holes bored straight into the ground. All dirt is often left piled near one entrance. There are often several openings to the burrow system, but these are usually plugged during the day. A burrow has separate food and sleeping chambers. Stores seeds in the food chamber to eat later. Fills the sleeping chamber with dried grass and sleeps in it, matting it down.

Not known to hibernate and often seen feeding year-round. If food becomes scarce due to drought, however, the pocket mouse may become inactive (torpid) for periods of time.

Feeds mainly on seeds (granivorous). Will gather larger seeds and transport them in its fur-lined cheek pouches, hence the common name "Pocket Mouse." These pouches are not inside the mouth, but are on the outside of the cheeks. Also eats insects when they are available (insectivorous).

Home ranges are very small, with most adults spending their entire life in an area less than 20 feet (6.1 m) wide. Males have a slightly larger territory than females. Some will reproduce throughout the year in Texas if enough food and water is available.

Similar species on next page **69**

Additional Pocket Mouse Species

Despite the common name "Mouse," pocket mice are not a type of mouse, nor are they closely related to any other mammal species in North America. Pocket mice are found only west of the Mississippi River, where they are mainly seen in open grassy fields and deserts. They live underground in burrows and prefer sandy soil, which allows them to dig more easily into the earth.

All pocket mice are nocturnal. They have coarse fur, often with stiff bristles, and fur-lined cheek pouches to carry food and nesting material—the reason for the term "Pocket" in their common names. The pouches are not inside their mouths, but rather on the outside of their cheeks.

Merriam's Pocket Mouse 2-2½"

Silky Pocket Mouse 2-2½"

Rock Pocket Mouse 2¾-3"

Nelson's Pocket Mouse 3-3¼"

Plains Pocket Mouse 3-4"

Chihuahuan Desert Pocket Mouse 3¼-4"

Mexican Spiny Pocket Mouse 4-4½"

Northern Grasshopper Mouse

Onychomys leucogaster

Family: Rats and Mice (Muridae)

Size: L 3–5" (7.5–13 cm); T 1–2¼" (2.5–5 cm)

Weight: ⅞–1⅞ oz. (25–53 g)

Description: Stout, thick-bodied mouse. Brown to gray above, white below. Large ears, often with a white patch in front of each ear. Short, thick bicolored tail, dark above, light below with a white tip. Tail is less than one-third the length of head and body.

Origin/Age: native; 1–2 years

Compare: Mearns' Grasshopper Mouse (pg. 75) has a shorter tail in proportion to its body. The White-footed Mouse (pg. 61) has a smaller body and a longer tail that lacks a white tip.

Habitat: grasslands, brushlands, fields with sandy soils

Home: nest of dried plant material, in a tunnel network with short escape tunnels; may take burrows of other small animals, plugs tunnels each morning to retain moisture and seal out predators

Food: omnivore; grasshoppers, beetles, caterpillars, and other insects; spiders, green plants, seeds, nuts, other small mammals including mice

Sounds: unusual high-pitched and drawn-out call, can be heard up to 50' (15 m); sharp dog-like bark when alarmed, defending territory or searching for mates, bark is similar to the barks and howls of a coyote, but is much quieter

Breeding: Feb–Aug mating; 28–32 days gestation

Young: 1–6 (average 3–4) pups 3–6 times per year; born naked with eyes closed

Signs: discarded insect parts such as wings and legs, network of aboveground runways leading to and from entrances to many small escape tunnels; scat not seen because this mouse defecates in underground chambers; can sometimes be heard vocalizing

Activity: nocturnal; active year-round, most active on moonless or overcast nights, may remain in nest during the coldest parts of winter or extremely hot parts of summer

Tracks: hind paw 1" (2.5 cm) long with 5 toes, forepaw ½" (1 cm) long with 4 toes

Stan's Notes: A stout-bodied mouse, good to have around due to its consumption of many insects. Fast and strong enough to take mammals of its own size, but feeds heavily on grasshoppers, hence the common name. Uses its short powerful legs to quickly maneuver and grab large insects, biting at the base of the head to kill or paralyze the prey before eating. When many grasshoppers are together, it grabs and bites one, immobilizing it, then drops it and repeats the process until all are dispatched.

Onychomys means "clawed mouse." Claws and its unusually long front toes help it manipulate large insects. The molars have very high cusps, allowing it to chew insect exoskeletons. Enlarged jaw muscles increase its biting and chewing power.

A predatory mammal, very territorial, marking scent posts with anal gland secretions. Dominant mice catch and kill subordinates that enter their territory. Pairs defend food, young, and home from other mice, predators, and even people.

Its courtship is complex for rodents and includes circling, mutual grooming, and sniffing before copulation. Fathers play a major role in raising young, which is not the case with other mice.

Additional Grasshopper Mouse Species

Only two of four grasshopper mice species are found in the state. The Mearns' Grasshopper Mouse (*O. arenicola*) is slightly smaller than the Northern and occurs only in the far western corner of Texas in the Trans-Pecos region.

Mearns' Grasshopper Mouse 3–4½"

Marsh Rice Rat
Oryzomys palustris

Family: Rats and Mice (Muridae)

Size: L 4½–5½" (11–14 cm); T 4–4½" (10–11 cm)

Weight: 1½–2½ oz. (43–71 g)

Description: Brown with grayish sides and off-white to gray below. Short wide snout. Small round ears. Dark eyes. Scaly tail, shorter than the length of body and head combined.

Origin/Age: native; 1–2 years

Compare: Much smaller than Black Rat (pg. 101), which has a naked tail longer than its head and body. Smaller than the cotton rats (pp. 87–91), with a more grizzled look and a larger, stockier body. The Coues' Rice Rat (pg. 79) is larger and found only in cattail bulrush resacas (oxbow lakes) in far southern Texas counties near Brownsville.

Habitat: usually associated with marshes and wetlands

Home: shallow burrow above high water levels or round nests made of dried grasses, sedges or other plants, usually under logs and other debris above high water, occasionally uses an old bird nest

Food: omnivore; seeds, nuts, insects, carrion, birds, bird eggs, small mammals

Sounds: usually silent; makes inconsequential noises

Breeding: year-round mating; 20–25 days gestation; female can mate within hours of giving birth

Young: 2–4 (average 3) offspring up to 6 times per year; born naked with eyes closed, eyes open at about 5–6 days, weaned at 2 weeks

Signs: water trails along the surface at the water's edge, cut plants, cut plants on feeding platforms in shallow water

Activity: nocturnal; active year-round, can be active on cloudy days

Tracks: hind paw 1" (2.5 cm) long with a narrow heel and 5 toes, forepaw ½" (1 cm) long with 4 well-spread toes; often follows the same paths over and over, making individual tracks difficult to distinguish

Stan's Notes: This is a small, semiaquatic native rat with a good disposition and habits. Not usually aggressive and does not enter homes or barns, staying mainly in wetlands where it feeds on green plants.

Swims underwater, searching for the tender parts of underwater plants. Also will eat aquatic insects, snails, and tiny crabs. Consumes equal amounts of plant and animal matter, the diet changing with the season and the season's abundance of food. Apparently has an affinity for cultivated rice, which accounts for its common name. This rat is so small and occurs in such low density, it usually never causes damage to crops or wetland plants.

Additional Rice Rat Species

There are only two rice rat species in Texas. Coues' Rice Rat (*O. couesi*), a Mexican species that reaches its northern limits in southern Texas, occurs only in wetlands with cattails near resacas (oxbow lakes) and only in two counties in the lower Rio Grande Valley. The Texas Parks and Wildlife Department regards this native rat as threatened because of

Coues' Rice Rat 5–5½"

its limited range and restricted habitat requirements. Loss of wetland habitat and drought are its biggest threat.

Ord's Kangaroo Rat
Dipodomys ordii

Family: Kangaroo Rats and Pocket Mice (Heteromyidae)

Size: L 4–6" (10–15 cm); T 4½–6" (11–15 cm)

Weight: 2–3 oz. (57–85 g)

Description: Unique rat with a big stocky body, long back legs and short front legs. Often stands up with front legs held against chest. Variable color, often yellow brown with a darker back and white chin, front legs, and belly. Large eyes. Dark mark over snout. Short round ears. White spot by eyes and ears. Tail longer than body, bicolored, large tuft at tip. Five toes on hind feet, fifth toe on the side of foot.

Origin/Age: native; 2–4 years

Compare: Merriam's Kangaroo Rat (pg. 85) has 4 toes on its hind feet. Banner-tailed Kangaroo Rat (pg. 85) is larger, with a white-tipped dark tail. Gulf Coast Kangaroo Rat (pg. 85) is much lighter in color.

Habitat: variety of habitats, sandy soils, deserts, grasslands, sagebrush

Home: network of tunnels, 2–3" (5–7.5 cm) wide and up to 6' (1.8 m) long, leading to inner chambers used for sleeping and feeding, often has several escape exits and dead-end tunnels for hiding

Food: herbivore, insectivore; seeds, nuts, insects

Sounds: low grunts, squeals, purrs; drums feet if excited

Breeding: year-round mating; 25–30 days gestation; young females become sexually mature at 2 months

Young: 1–6 (average 4) offspring 2 times per year, as weather permits; born naked with eyes closed

81

five toes

Signs: burrows in sandy soils, sometimes with well-worn trails leading away; often seen on dirt roads at night within the path of vehicle headlights

Activity: nocturnal; active year-round, remains in burrow during rain or on very cold nights

Tracks: hind paw 1¾" (4.5 cm) long with a narrow heel and 5 toes, forepaw 1¼" (3 cm) long with 4 well-spread toes; often follows the same paths over and over, making individual tracks difficult to distinguish, but often has a tail drag mark

Stan's Notes: A distinctive and attractive rodent, hard to confuse with other types of rats or mice. It has five toes on its hind feet, which can help to identify. Will hop on its hind feet (bipedal) like a kangaroo, hence the common name, but also walks on all four legs. When standing still, holds its front legs tightly against its chest and uses its long tail for balance and support. Uses its front feet to gather and hold seeds to eat or places them in its cheek pouches for transporting back to the burrow.

Can be approached at night, but when disturbed it will leap and quickly run with a zigzag pattern back to the burrow to escape, thumping its hind feet at the burrow entrance before diving in for safety. Digs its own burrow, which has several entrances, interconnecting tunnels and many chambers for sleeping, food storage and waste. Solitary animals, with only one individual living in each burrow system. Blocks the entrances with sand and other plant material during the day to maintain temperature and humidity, and for safety.

There is an oil-secreting gland between its shoulders, which serves to distinguish individuals and sexes. To prevent from becoming oily and matted, it takes dust baths or sand baths regularly, rolling around on the ground to coat its fur with oil-absorbing dirt.

Most individuals can survive without drinking water, obtaining water directly from seed digestion. Will drink from surface water if available.

Similar species on next page **83**

Of the 17 kangaroo rat species in the United States, 5 are in Texas. These rats are some of the most easily identified rodents. They have silky fur, large eyes, distinctive white markings and long tails with a bushy tuft at the tip. They stand or rest on their hind legs with front feet tucked against their chests, and hop on their back feet (bipedal), but walk on all fours. Kangaroo rats are seed eaters, carrying seeds to their burrows in their cheek pouches.

The Gulf Coast Kangaroo Rat occurs in south Texas and the Padre Islands, where it can be abundant. At night it can be seen scurrying around sand dunes on well-worn paths. It has five toes on its hind feet and is lighter in color than the similar Ord's Kangaroo Rat.

The Texas Kangaroo Rat is a large four-toed rat with a distinctive white-tipped tail. Limited to a few counties in north central Texas, it is a fairly uncommon species that lives in clay soils with short grasses and mesquite bushes.

Merriam's Kangaroo Rat lives in the deserts of the Trans-Pecos in western Texas and south along the border. It tolerates a wider variety of habitat than the other kangaroo rats that live in sandy, rocky soils, where seed-producing plants are sparse.

The Banner-tailed Kangaroo Rat is the largest kangaroo rat in Texas, measuring over a foot long with its tail. This species builds large mounds approximately 12 inches (30 cm) tall and 10 feet (3 m) wide. Communicates with other Bannertails by drumming its hind feet while sitting on mounds. Found in sandy and rocky soils in far western Texas, with limited distribution.

Gulf Coast Kangaroo Rat (gray morph) 3¾–4"

Gulf Coast Kangaroo Rat (tan morph) 3¾–4"

Texas Kangaroo Rat 4½–4¾"

Merriam's Kangaroo Rat 4½–5"

Banner-tailed Kangaroo Rat 5¼–6½"

Hispid Cotton Rat
Sigmodon hispidus

Family: Rats and Mice (Muridae)

Size: L 6–8½" (15–21.5 cm); T 4–5" (10–13 cm)

Weight: 3–5 oz. (85–142 g)

Description: Large-bodied rat. Dark grizzled back and rump, lighter sides, and a grayish white belly. Cream eye-ring and small dark eyes. Round ears. Short stout snout. Tail is dark gray above, sparsely haired, and slightly shorter than head and body.

Origin/Age: native; 1–4 years

Compare: Larger than Yellow-nosed Cotton Rat (pg. 91), which has a distinctive yellowish snout and is found only in a narrow area in the Trans-Pecos region. Tawny-bellied Cotton Rat (pg. 91) has a tawny belly and is very uncommon, reported only from isolated areas near Fort Davis.

Habitat: wide variety from desert scrub to dense grasslands, almost always near water or wet areas

Home: network of tunnels, 2–3" (5–7.5 cm) wide and up to 6' (1.8 m) long, leading to inner chambers used for sleeping and feeding, often has several escape exits and dead-end tunnels for hiding

Food: herbivore; leaves, seeds, nuts

Sounds: inconsequential; high-pitched squeaks, squeals

Breeding: year-round mating; 25–27 days gestation; female can mate within hours of giving birth

Young: 2–12 (average 6) offspring up to 5 times per year; born well furred and well developed with eyes closed, eyes open at about 60 hours, able to walk and run after birth, weaned at 1–2 weeks

Signs: nests made with plant material aboveground and below, well-worn runways in grass

Activity: nocturnal, crepuscular; active year-round, can be active on cloudy days

Tracks: hind paw 1½" (4 cm) long with a narrow heel and 5 toes, forepaw 1" (2.5 cm) long with 4 well-spread toes; often follows the same paths over and over, making individual tracks difficult to distinguish when it has been walking

Stan's Notes: One of three species of cotton rats found in Texas, all looking very similar with a stocky body, short round snout, coarse grizzled fur and a pleasant disposition. Hispid Cotton Rat is one of the largest cotton rats and is the most common species, found in every county in the state.

Cotton rats are active year-round and can be active at any time of day, depending on weather. During rainy years they reproduce much more, with a marked decrease in reproduction during drought years.

Nests are either in chambers underground or aboveground in dense clumps of grass. Similar to harvest mice, the aboveground nests are ball-shaped masses of dried plant material.

Main food is green grass and when available, seeds. This rat will also feed on insects and the eggs of ground-nesting birds.

Marks territories with scents indicating sex, dominance, and sexually readiness. Also uses visual signals, such as body postures, to communicate between individuals.

Can breed up to 5 times a year in the wild and up to 10 times a year in captivity. Females often breed shortly after giving birth. Becomes sexually mature in 40 days. Young rats look different from their parents until they reach 6 months. Only the females care for the young.

The common name "Hispid," originating from Latin, refers to its dark, grizzled, stiff hairs and accurately describes the appearance of this tame and timid critter. An important source of food for many predators such as bobcats, coyotes, hawks, eagles, falcons, and just about anything that can catch them.

Similar species on next page **89**

Cotton rats are a unique group of large rodents with short round snouts and distinctive coarse fur, appearing somewhat like large voles. They live in grassy habitats, feeding mainly on green plants. In areas of activity, they make runways through the grass.

There are four cotton rat species, three of which are seen in Texas. Yellow-nosed Cotton Rat is one of the smallest species and has an orange-to-yellow patch around its nose. This rat is isolated in just a few counties in the far western corner of the state.

The Tawny-bellied Cotton Rat has a tan or tawny belly unlike the white bellies of the other cotton rat species. The Hispid Cotton Rat has the largest range in the United States, from the Carolinas to Florida and west across all of Texas. Chances are if you are seeing a cotton rat in Texas, it will be the Hispid.

Yellow-nosed
Cotton Rat
6–7½"

Tawny-bellied
Cotton Rat 6–7½"

Southern Plains Woodrat
Neotoma micropus

Family: Rats and Mice (Muridae)

Size: L 7¼–8" (18.5–20 cm); T 6–7" (15–18 cm)

Weight: 8½–9½ oz. (241–269 g)

Description: Large mouse-like rat, gray with tan highlights and a white chin, chest, and belly. Long pointed snout. Large ears. Large dark eyes. Tail is shorter than the body, sharply bicolored, dark above, sparsely furred, and lacking a tufted tip.

Origin/Age: native; 1–3 years

Compare: The Mexican Woodrat (pg. 97) occurs in rocky canyons and higher elevations. Eastern Woodrat (pg. 97) is only in the eastern third of Texas in forest and river bottoms. Eastern White-throated Woodrat (pg. 97) is in western Texas. Black Rat (pg. 101) has a naked tail and lacks a white chin.

Habitat: desert scrub, brushlands, mesquite, coniferous and juniper forests, foothills

Home: small debris pile or very large nest of many sticks, branches, bones, and more (midden), chamber lined with dry vegetation, by a large cactus, tree, log, or in a building, with many entrances, used by many individual rats over time

Food: herbivore; wide variety of green plants, mainly cacti, grasses, seeds, berries, very few insects

Sounds: thumping or drumming created by the hind feet

Breeding: year-round mating; 25–35 days gestation

Young: 2–4 (average 3) offspring up to 1–2 times per year; born naked with eyes closed, opening at 15 days, weaned at 62–72 days

Signs: large dome-shaped stick house (midden), reminiscent of a brush pile, containing hundreds of sticks, bark, bones, and whatever else the animal is able to carry, well-worn trails leading out and away from the midden in many directions

Activity: nocturnal; active year-round, can be active on cloudy days

Tracks: hind paw 1½" (4 cm) long with a narrow heel and 5 toes, forepaw ⅞" (2.3 cm) long with 4 well-spread toes; frequently follows the same paths over and over, making individual tracks difficult to distinguish when it has been hopping

Stan's Notes: Southern Plains Woodrat is the most widespread of all species of woodrats occurring in Texas. Almost always associated with cactus or thorny desert shrubs and usually never associated with rocks. Often called Pack Rat because of its habit of collecting sticks, bark, bones, and even shiny metal or mineral objects that it stores in and around its den, called a midden. Digs a network of tunnels beneath the midden, especially if there is a limited supply of building materials and the midden is small.

Often builds its nest underneath a particularly large prickly pear cactus, yucca, or cholla. Will also nest at the base of a large tree, next to a fallen log or inside an abandoned building. Not a social animal, with only one individual or a mother with young living in each nest. Many middens may be found in close proximity, within 30–50 feet (9.1–15 m), each occupied by an individual.

Normally nocturnal, but sometimes can be seen out and about on a cloudy day. Communicates by striking its hind feet on the ground, creating a thumping or drumming sound. Eats mainly cactus plants and fruit.

Young are born with front teeth that permit them to grasp their mother's nipple and not let go. If the mother starts walking while nursing, the young will continue to clench and end up getting dragged behind her, bouncing along the ground on their backs.

Similar species on next page

Woodrats are large rats that look like Deer Mice (pg. 64) on steroids. They all have well-furred, bicolored tails and white hind feet. They make their homes from sticks and debris including junk from garbage, which is the reason for their other common name, Pack Rat.

All woodrats are solitary and territorial. Other woodrat species in Texas are more restricted in their ranges than the Southern Plains Woodrat. Eastern White-throated Woodrat occurs in the western half of Texas. The Mexican Woodrat is seen only at high elevations above 5,000 feet (1,525 m). Eastern Woodrat is found in the eastern third of the state.

Eastern White-throated Woodrat 8–8½"

Mexican Woodrat 8–10"

Eastern Woodrat 7¼–11½"

Norway Rat
Rattus norvegicus

Family: Rats and Mice (Muridae)

Size: L 8–10" (20–25 cm); T 5–8" (13–20 cm)

Weight: ½–1 lb. (0.2–0.5 kg)

Description: Brown to grayish brown above and gray below. Long narrow snout. Large round ears. Dark eyes. Scaly tail, shorter than the body length.

Origin/Age: non-native; 2–4 years

Compare: Black Rat (pg. 101) has a longer tail than its head and body combined. Larger than all mice, voles (except muskrats), and shrews. Larger than most woodrats (pp. 93–97), which all have well-furred tails. Most cotton rats (pp. 87–91) are smaller, with a more grizzled look. Look for large ears and a long naked tail that is shorter than the head and body length to help identify.

Habitat: cities, dumps, homes, farms

Home: network of tunnels, 2–3" (5–7.5 cm) wide and up to 6' (1.8 m) long, with inner chambers for sleeping and feeding, often has several escape exits and dead-end tunnels for hiding

Food: omnivore; seeds, nuts, insects, carrion, birds, bird eggs, small mammals

Sounds: high-pitched squeaks if squabbling with other rats; scratching, gnawing, or scampering at night

Breeding: year-round mating; 20–25 days gestation; female can mate within hours of giving birth

Young: 2–9 (average 6) offspring up to 10 times per year; born naked with eyes closed, eyes open at about 2 weeks, weaned at 3–4 weeks

Signs: holes chewed in barn walls or doors, well-worn paths along walls or that lead in and out of chewed holes, smell of urine near the nest site; large, hard, cylindrical, dark brown-to-black droppings, deposited along trails

scat

Activity: nocturnal; active year-round, can be active on cloudy days

Tracks: hind paw 1½" (4 cm) long with a narrow heel and 5 toes, forepaw 1" (2.5 cm) long with 4 well-spread toes; often follows the same paths over and over, making individual tracks difficult to distinguish

Stan's Notes: Benefits from its association with people, feeding on discarded food and carrion in cities and stored grain on farms.

Also called Common Rat, Brown Rat, House Rat, Water Rat, and Sewer Rat. A good swimmer and climber. Tolerates cold and hot temperatures well. Digs by loosening dirt with its front feet, pushes dirt under its belly, then turns and pushes the dirt out with its head and front feet. Chews through roots if in the way. A true omnivore and sometimes predatory, killing chickens and other small farm animals. Able to reproduce quickly when food is abundant.

Has a small territory with a high population density. Migrates on occasion. Large numbers may leave an area, presumably due to overcrowding and a dwindling food supply. Can be aggressive if backed into a corner or during a run-in with the family dog.

First scientifically described in Norway, but thought to come from central Asia. Introduced via trading ships in the 1600–1700s.

The same species as white lab rats. A carrier of disease and fleas, it should be exterminated when possible. Hard to trap because of its escape exits. Due to intense eradication efforts (artificial selection), it has become resistant to many types of rat poisons.

Additional Rat Species

Black Rat (*R. rattus*), a species from Asia, was introduced to America in the early 1500s. Also called House Rat or Roof Rat, it is the famed species that carried bubonic plague. A climber, seen in barn rafters and running on power lines. Less common than Norway Rat and found only in the southern half of Texas.

Black Rat
6 ¼–7 ½"

Woodland Vole
Microtus pinetorum

Family: Rats and Mice (Muridae)

Size: L 3¾–4½" (9.5–11 cm); T ½–1¼" (1–3 cm)

Weight: ¾–1¼ oz. (21–35 g)

Description: Overall chestnut brown fur with a glossy or shiny appearance and gray chest and belly. Short blunt snout. Tiny eyes. Small ears, but visible. Short bicolored tail, changing gradually from dark on top to light below.

Origin/Age: native; 1–2 years

Compare: The Prairie Vole (pg. 107) has a more grizzled appearance, with longer, black-tipped fur and a sharply bicolored tail. Prairie Vole occurs only in two counties in far northern Texas. Mexican Vole (pg. 107) is darker and is found only in the higher parts of the Guadalupe Mountains.

Habitat: deciduous forests with thick leaf litter and green ground cover, dense grass patches

Home: ball-shaped nest with a hollow center, made of dried grasses, often belowground in a network of tunnels; lives mainly underground, also maintains a series of surface tunnels

Food: herbivore; green plants in summer; roots, bulbs, seeds, berries, and other fruit in winter

Sounds: inconsequential; chatters with up to 5 notes per call when threatened

Breeding: Feb–Oct mating; 20–24 days gestation

Young: 1–4 pups up to 4 times per year; born with eyes and ears closed, weaned at 17 days

Signs: well-worn runways and tunnels through thick vegetation

Activity: nocturnal, diurnal; active year-round, often active 24 hours, with several hours of rest followed by several hours of activity

Tracks: hind paw ⅝" (1.5 cm) long with 5 toes, forepaw ¼" (0.6 cm) long with 4 toes; individual tracks are indistinguishable and create a single groove

Stan's Notes: A vole of deciduous forests that have a thick layer of decaying leaves and branches (duff). Sometimes called Pine Vole, which is somewhat of a misnomer since it does not spend much time in coniferous habitats. The Latin species name *pinetorum* is misleading since it refers to a pine habitat. Why these names have been applied is unknown. The genus name Microtus is Greek and refers to the small ears that are common to this genus.

The small body and ears, tiny eyes, and large front claws suit it well for an underground (fossorial) life of digging. Digs out areas to cache food for consumption later.

The chestnut color, small size, and unique tail help to identify the Woodland Vole. Its bicolored tail is unlike the tail of any other vole species, gradually changing from dark above to light below.

Can be semi-colonial, with several families sharing a single nest chamber. Doesn't seem to have the "peak and crash" population cycles common to the other vole species. Owls, hawks, coyotes, foxes, minks and other predators all depend on these critters for a constant source of food.

Similar species on next page

Additional Vole Species

All three vole species in Texas have stocky bodies, blunt noses, and naked tails. None of them are abundant or common. They usually have dark fur and, except for the Muskrat (pg. 109), very short tails.

Voles are considered an essential component of many ecosystems in the state, with larger mammals and birds of prey relying on healthy populations of voles as a food source. In some vole species, populations rise and fall dramatically from year to year in fairly predictable cycles. Low populations of voles can cause raptors and other predators to move to areas where populations are higher.

Voles occur in open areas and leave obvious signs of activity such as runways through grass, cut grass stems, and piles of half-eaten grass and other plants. Most are active on the surface of the ground, retreating to underground burrows to sleep and rest. They remain active year-round even in areas of the country where winter is severe.

The Prairie Vole is found only in two counties in the far northern part of the state. Mexican Vole occurs only in the higher parts of the Guadalupe Mountains.

Prairie Vole 4–5"

Mexican Vole 3¾–5½"

Muskrat
Ondatra zibethicus

Family: Rats and Mice (Muridae)

Size: L 8–12" (20–30 cm); T 7–12" (18–30 cm)

Weight: 1–4 lb. (0.5–1.8 kg)

Description: Glossy dark brown, lighter on the sides and belly. Long naked tail, covered with scales and slightly vertically flattened (taller than it is wide). Small round ears. Tiny eyes.

Origin/Age: native; 3–10 years

Compare: Muskrat has a longer, thinner tail than American Beaver (pg. 117), which is much larger and has a large flat tail.

Habitat: ponds, lakes, ditches, small rivers, streams

Home: small den, called a lodge, made of cattail leaves and other soft green (herbaceous) plant material, 1–2 underwater entrances, often has 1 chamber, sometimes a burrow in a lakeshore, larger dens may have 2 chambers with separate occupants

Food: herbivore, carnivore to a much lesser extent; aquatic plants, roots, cattail and bulrush shoots, roots, and rhizomes; also eats dead fish, crayfish, clams, snails, and baby birds

Sounds: inconsequential; chewing sounds can be heard when feeding above water on feeding platform

Breeding: Apr–Aug mating, year-round in some areas; 25–30 days gestation

Young: 6–7 offspring 2–3 times per year; born naked with eyes closed, swims at about 2 weeks, weaned at about 3 weeks

swimming

lodge

Signs: well-worn trails through vegetation along a shore near a muskrat lodge, feeding platform made of floating plant material, 24" square (154.8 sq. cm), usually strewn with partially eaten cattails and other plants; lodge made of mud and cut vegetation, occasionally many lodges will dot the surface of a shallow lake

Activity: nocturnal, crepuscular; active all year, doesn't hibernate

Tracks: hind paw 2½–3½" (6–9 cm) long with 5 toes and a long heel, forepaw about half the size with 5 toes spread evenly; hind paws fall near or onto fore prints (direct register) when walking, often obliterating the forepaw tracks; prints may show only 4 toes since the fifth toe is not well formed, often has a tail drag mark

Stan's Notes: A member of the Voles and Lemmings (Arvicolinae) subfamily, which is in the Rats and Mice (Muridae) family. Native only to North America; introduced all over the world. The musky odor (most evident in males during breeding season) emanating from two glands near the base of its rat-like tail is the reason for the common name. Some say the common name is a derivation of the Algonquian word *musquash*, which sounds somewhat like "muskrat."

Mostly aquatic, the muskrat is highly suited to living in water. It has a waterproof coat that protects it from frigid temperatures. Partially webbed hind feet and a fringe of hair along each toe help propel the animal. The tail, which is slightly flattened vertically, also helps with forward motion and is used as a rudder. Its mouth can close behind the front teeth only, allowing the animal to cut vegetation free while it is submerged.

A good swimmer that swims backward and sideways with ease. Able to stay submerged for up to 15 minutes. Surfaces to eat. May store some roots and tubers in mud below the water to consume during winter.

It lives with other muskrats in small groups, but there is no social structure and individuals act mainly on their own. Becomes sexually mature the first spring after its birth.

Lodge building seems to concentrate in the fall. Not all muskrats construct a mound-type lodge. Many dig a burrow in a shore. A muskrat lodge is not like a beaver lodge, which is made with woody plant material. There is only one beaver lodge per lake or stream, while there are often several muskrat lodges in a body of water. Does not defecate in the lodge, so the interior living space of the lodge is kept remarkably clean.

Overcrowding can occur in fall and winter, causing individuals to travel great distances in spring to establish new homes. Many muskrats are killed when crossing roads during this season.

Nutria
Myocaster coypus

Family: Myocastorids (Myocastoridae)

Size: L 15–37" (38–94 cm); T 11–18" (28–45 cm)

Weight: 14–18 lb. (6.3–8.1 kg)

Description: Light to dark brown with gold highlights. Slightly lighter belly. Long, round scaly tail. Round dark ears, long stout snout, small eyes, and white chin Large orange incisors. Short legs. Female has a row of mammae on each side of the back.

Origin/Age: non-native; 3–10 years

Compare: Muskrat (pg. 109) is smaller and thinner, with a smaller snout. American Beaver (pg. 117) has a large flat tail.

Habitat: ponds, wetlands, ditches, small rivers

Home: shallow burrow, single chamber, often in a wetland bank, sometimes in a tangle of tree roots, entrance above water line; nest of cattail leaves and other soft green plant (herbaceous) materials on land or in thick vegetation near the water; sometimes takes over an old beaver or muskrat lodge

Food: herbivore; aquatic plants, roots, cattail and bulrush shoots, sedges, roots, rhizomes; along the coast it feeds on shellfish

Sounds: chorus of pig-like grunts heard along wetlands at dusk; makes chewing sounds when eating on a feeding platform

Breeding: all year in most of Texas; 125–135 days gestation

Young: 2–11 (usually 5) offspring 2–3 times per year; born fully furred with eyes open, able to move around and feed within hours

Signs: well-worn trails through vegetation along wetlands, feeding platform constructed of floating plant material, 24" square (154.8 sq. cm), usually strewn with partially eaten cattails and other plants; nests made of cut vegetation; elongated scat found on feeding platforms or in shallow water

Activity: nocturnal; active year-round, does not hibernate

Tracks: hind paw 4½–5½" (10.5–14 cm) long with 5 toes (webbed) and a long heel, forepaw about half the size with 5 toes spread evenly; hind paws fall near fore prints when walking; hind prints may show only 4 toes since the fifth toe is not well formed and off to the side; may have a tail drag mark

Stan's Notes: A large aquatic rodent, nearly the size of a beaver. Introduced from South America in 1889 for its high-quality fur. Raised on ranches for its fur, it eventually escaped into the wild due to a variety of reasons. During the 1940s the fur industry collapsed and many others were released into the wild.

Originally from semiaquatic habitats in southern Chile and farther south in Tierra del Fuego. One of the few mammals that can thrive in fresh water and saltwater. Today in Texas it has spread east to west starting on the Gulf coast, moving west as far as Big Bend National Park, and north into the panhandle. Reported in 22 states total, but occurs mainly in Gulf coast states.

An excellent swimmer, with only its ears, eyes, and nostrils visible above the surface. Can dive and remained submerged for long periods of time to evade predators.

Competes with the smaller, local native muskrat species for the limited suitable habitats such as wetlands. Lives in a variety of homes including burrows that it digs itself or takes from others. Feeds, loafs, gives birth, and escapes from predators on circular platforms constructed of vegetation, which are often mistaken for muskrat houses.

Breeds year-round and quickly overpopulates. Once established, it often eats most of the aquatic vegetation, causing extensive damage to wetlands. Eats all of the native vegetation that holds wetland soils together. A nocturnal animal, so usually only the damage is seen, not the culprit.

Considered an invasive species in the United States. Previously sold as a "natural" control for noxious weeds, this unfortunately also helped extend its range in nearly all states where it occurs. Efforts to control the population include government-sponsored programs to hunt and trap the animal. While South Americans enjoy its meat, efforts here to market it for consumption did not catch on with the public.

American Beaver
Castor canadensis

Family: Beavers (Castoridae)

Size: L 3–4' (0.9–1.2 m); T 7–14" (18–36 cm)

Weight: 20–60 lb. (9–27 kg)

Description: Reddish brown fur. Body often darker than head. Large, flat, naked black tail, covered with scales. Small round ears. Large, exposed orange incisors. Tiny eyes.

Origin/Age: native; 10–15 years

Compare: Much larger than Muskrat (pg. 109), which has a long narrow tail. Look for a large flat tail to help identify the American Beaver.

Habitat: rivers, streams, ponds, lakes, ditches, wherever trees and water are present

Home: den, called a lodge, hollow inside with holes on top for ventilation, 1–2 underwater entrances; beavers that live on rivers often dig burrows in riverbanks rather than constructing dens

Food: herbivore; soft bark, inner bark, aquatic plants, green leaves

Sounds: loud slap created by hitting the surface of water with the tail before diving when alarmed, chewing or gnawing sounds when feeding or felling trees

Breeding: Jan–Mar mating; 120 days gestation

Young: 1–8 kits once per year; about 1 lb. (0.5 kg); born well furred with eyes open, able to swim within 1 week

tail slap

lodge

Signs: dam and lodge made from large woody branches can indicate current or former activity since structures remain well after the beaver has moved on or been killed, chewed tree trunks with large amounts of wood chips at the base of trees, flattened paths through vegetation lead-

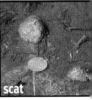

scat

ing to and from a lake; oval pellets, 1" (2.5 cm) long, containing sawdust-like material and bark, scat seldom on land

Activity: nocturnal, crepuscular; active year-round

Tracks: hind paw 5" (13 cm) long with 5 toes pointing forward and a long narrow heel, forepaw 3" (7.5 cm) with 5 splayed toes; wide tail drag mark often wipes out paw prints

Stan's Notes: Largest member of the Rodentia order in Texas. Body is well suited for swimming. Valves close off the ears and nostrils when underwater, and a clear membrane covers the eyes. Can remain submerged up to 15 minutes. Webbed toes on hind feet help it swim as fast as 6 mph (10 km/h). Special lips seal the mouth yet leave the front incisors exposed, allowing it to carry branches in its mouth without water getting inside. At the lodge, it eats the soft bark of smaller branches the same way we eat corn on the cob. Doesn't eat the interior wood. Stores branches for later use by sticking them in mud on a lake or river bottom.

Has a specialized claw on each hind foot that is split like a comb and is used for grooming. Secretes a pungent oily substance (castor) from glands near the base of its tail. Castor is used to mark territories or boundaries called castor mounds.

Monogamous and mates for life. However, will take a new mate if partner is lost. Can live up to 20 years in captivity.

Young remain with parents through their first winter. They help cut and store a winter food source and maintain the dam while parents raise another set of young. Young disperse at 2 years.

Builds a dam to back up a large volume of water, creating a pond. Cuts trees at night by gnawing trunks. Uses larger branches to construct the dam and lodge. Cuts smaller branches and twigs of felled trees into 6-foot (1.8 m) sections. Dam repair is triggered by the sound of moving water, not by sight. Most repair activity takes place at night.

No other mammal except people changes its environment as much as beavers. Frogs, turtles, and many bird species, including ducks, herons, and egrets, benefit from the newly created habitat. Beaver ponds play an important role in moose populations in other areas where moose live. Moose feed on aquatic plants, cool themselves, and escape biting insects in summer in beaver ponds.

Brazilian Free-tailed Bat

Tadarida braziliensis

Family: Bats (Molossidae)

Size: L 2¼–2½" (5.5–6 cm); T 1¼–1½" (3–4 cm)

Weight: ¼–⅜ oz. (7–11 g)

Description: Overall brown fur with darker, naked wing membranes and a long tail that extends beyond the tail membrane. Very large, dark naked ears, not joined at the midline of the forehead. Bright black eyes. Pointed snout with vertical grooves in upper lips.

Origin/Age: native; 15–20 years

Compare: Few distinctive markings. Look for the uniform brown fur, long tail free from the membrane and large ears to help identify. Millions visit caves and mine shafts in summer, creating a spectacle when they leave the roost each evening.

Habitat: wide variety such as deciduous forests, suburban areas

Home: wide variety of roosts including tunnels, caves, old wells, hollow trees, attics of homes, churches, barns and other buildings, bridges, mine shafts

Food: insectivore; small to large flying insects

Sounds: rapid series of high-pitched clicking noises, high-pitched squeaks of pups calling persistently to mother after she leaves to feed can be heard from a distance up to 30' (9.1 m) away

Breeding: occurs in spring before arriving in Texas; 90–95 days gestation

Young: 1 pup per year, June to early July; born breach and naked with eyes closed, weighs one-third the weight of mother, flies at 28–35 days

121

Signs: piles of dark brown-to-black scat under roosting sites

Activity: nocturnal; active only on warm dry nights, comes out approximately 30 minutes after sunset, feeds until full, roosts the rest of night, returns to daytime roost before sunrise

Tracks: none

Stan's Notes: The official flying mammal of the state of Texas. A common bat seen in many habitats from desert to forest, cities to country. Millions arrive in spring after wintering in Mexico and Central and South America, and take up residency in tunnels, caves, homes, under bridges, and at other places providing a dark comfortable roost. In east Texas they inhabit old buildings and other structures and do not migrate. The world's largest colony of these bats occurs in Bracken Cave, near New Braunfels, along the southeastern edge of the Hill Country, which hosts as many as 20–40 million individuals in summer. In Austin, the Congress Avenue Bridge hosts a colony of 2.5 million bats during summer and is a major tourist attraction of the city.

Studies show that this bat feeds on many crop and forest pests and insects, making it a very beneficial animal to have around. It is estimated to eat 11–20 tons (10–18 mt) of insects annually.

A fast-flying bat, reaching speeds of 25 mph (40 km/h), with an erratic flight pattern, evident as it swoops and dives for beetles, mosquitoes, and other flying insects. Often forages over rivers and lakes, beneath streetlights or wherever large groups of flying insects congregate. Emits a high-frequency (27–48 kHz) sound (inaudible to people) to locate prey and listens for returning echoes (echolocation). Most of these bats catch and eat one insect every three seconds, consuming $\frac{1}{10}$ ounce (3 g) per hour. During summer, when rapidly growing pups demand increasing amounts of milk, a lactating female can consume up to $\frac{7}{10}$ ounce (20 g) of insects every night, which is nearly equal to her own body weight.

A mother does not carry her pups during flight, but leaves them clinging to the roost until she returns. Holds pups to her chest under a wing to nurse. Recognizes young by their vocalizations.

Homeowners frequently discover these bats when remodeling or adding onto their homes during winter months. Any unwanted bat found in homes should be professionally moved or removed to avoid hurting the animal.

Similar species on next page   **123**

There are 43 bat species in the United States, with 33 species in Texas—more than in any other state in the country. The order of bats, called Chiroptera, means "hand wing" and refers to the elongated fingers that all bats have with thin membranous skin stretched between. No other mammal besides the bat has the ability to fly.

All bats are nocturnal, with small eyes and large ears. They use high-frequency ultrasonic sounds (outside the hearing range of people) to avoid obstacles and find insect prey while in flight.

Bats live in all of the temperate regions in the world except for the polar regions. In Texas, the Big Bend region of the Trans-Pecos supports 18 kinds of bats—more than in other parts of the state. This region also supports some of the most uncommon or rare bats in the state.

Eastern Pipistrelle
2–2¼"

Evening Bat
1¾–2¾"

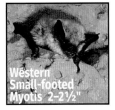

Western Small-footed Myotis 2–2½"

Fringed Myotis
2–2¾"

Western Pipistrelle
2–2¾"

Big Brown Bat 2–3"

Silver-haired Bat
2–3"

Eastern Red Bat
2–3"

California Myotis 2–3"

Ghost-faced Bat
2¼–2¾"

Townsend's Big-eared Bat
2¼–3"

Spotted Bat
2½–3"

Yuma Myotis
2½–3"

Hoary Bat
2–4"

Hairy-legged Vampire Bat
2¾–3¼"

Similar species on next page **125**

Pocketed Free-tailed Bat 3–3¼"

Mexican Long-nosed Bat 3–3½"

Mexican Long-tongued Bat 3–3½"

Long-legged Myotis 3–3½"

Western Red Bat 3¼–3¾"

Southeastern Myotis 3¼–3⅞"

Cave Myotis 3½–4"

Pallid Bat 3¾–4"

Western Yellow Bat 3¾–4"

Rafinesque's Big-eared Bat 3⅞–4¼"

Northern Yellow Bat 4–4½"

Seminole Bat 4¼–4½"

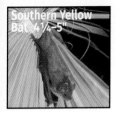

Southern Yellow Bat 4¼–5"

Big Free-tailed Bat 4⅞–5½"

Western Bonneted Bat 5–5¼"

Gray-footed Chipmunk
Tamias canipes

Family: Squirrels (Sciuridae)

Size: L 4¾–5¼" (12–13.5 cm); T 3–4½" (7.5–11 cm)

Weight: 2–3 oz. (57–85 g)

Description: Overall brown fur with alternating dark and light stripes from nose to base of tail. Orange brown sides with gray nape, shoulders, and rump. Pale brown stripes on face and through eyes. Gray on top of hind feet. Whitish belly. Long orange brown tail, nearly the length of the body, often dark-tipped.

Origin/Age: native; 2–4 years

Compare: No other chipmunk species occurs in Texas. Best to use location and elevation to help identify the Gray-footed.

Habitat: forests, coniferous woods between 6,000–8,500' (1,830–2,590 m)

Home: burrow, entrance usually a small round hole with no trace of excavated dirt, often under a fallen log or under a large rock, occasionally nests in a tree or old woodpecker hole, may have different burrows in summer and winter

Food: omnivore; seeds, fruit, nuts, insects, fungi, buds, flowers, frogs, baby birds, bird eggs, small snakes

Sounds: distinctive high-pitched series of "chip" and "chuck" notes that sound like a small bird

Breeding: Apr–May mating; 28–30 days gestation

Young: 4–6 offspring 1–2 times per year; born naked with eyes closed, weaned at about 40–45 days

Signs: piles of peeled cones and acorns and other seeds on a log or large rock; oblong dark brown pellets, ⅛" (0.3 cm) long, often not seen and not key in identifying this species

Activity: diurnal; doesn't come out on cold rainy days, seen running on the forest floor

Tracks: hind paw 1¼" (3 cm) long with 5 toes, forepaw with 4 toes is about half the size of hind paw; 1 set of 4 tracks; hind paws fall in front of fore prints; tracks rarely seen since it lives in a dry rocky habitat

Stan's Notes: The only chipmunk species in Texas. Found mainly in higher elevations of the Sierra Diablo and Guadalupe Mountains in the Trans-Pecos region (Culberson County) between 6,000–8,500 feet (1,830–2,590 m). Occurs mostly in coniferous forests in the high elevations of Texas and New Mexico only. Seems to prefer downed logs or rock crevices close to forest edges, where it can quickly escape any danger. Its hind feet are topped with gray, hence the common name.

Like other chipmunks, this species has fur-lined internal cheek pouches for carrying food or dirt and other items while it digs tunnels. Feeds mainly on Douglas fir pine cone seeds and acorns, but also consumes mushrooms, insects, and berries. Comfortable climbing trees to gather seeds, buds, and flowers for food. Most spend the day foraging for seeds and cones on the forest floor.

Usually solitary. Most active in early morning and late afternoon. Sometimes makes its home in an old woodpecker cavity. Stores large amounts of seeds, nuts, and dried berries in an underground cavity. Feeds on its cache when it is not outside due to weather. Hibernates for short periods of time, waking to feed, and can be also seen aboveground on warm, sunny winter days.

In late winter the males emerge several weeks before the females. Once the females emerge, mating follows shortly afterward. Males will compete for females, but both males and females mate with several mates per season.

The home range or territory is approximately ½–1 acre (0.2–0.4 ha), with parts of one territory overlapping onto others. Males have larger territories than the females.

Matures sexually at 10–12 months. Breeding season begins in late April to early May and lasts only a few weeks.

Southern Flying Squirrel
Glaucomys volans

Family: Squirrels (Sciuridae)

Size: L 5–7" (13–18 cm); T 3–5" (7.5–13 cm)

Weight: 1½–2½ oz. (43–71 g)

Description: Light brown-to-gray fur above. White underside. Wide flat tail, gray above and white below. Large, bulging dark eyes. Loose fold of skin between the front and hind legs.

Origin/Age: native; 2–5 years

Compare: The flying squirrel is the only nocturnal squirrel. Can be identified by the wide flat tail and large bulging eyes.

Habitat: large trees, along rivers and streams, woodlands, urban and suburban yards and parks, prefers hummocks where Spanish moss is abundant

Home: nest lined with soft plant material, usually in an old woodpecker hole, sometimes in a nest box or an attic in homes and outbuildings, may build a small round nest of leaves on a tree branch; nest is similar to that of the Eastern Gray Squirrel (pg. 157), only smaller

Food: omnivore; seeds, nuts, carrion, baby mice, baby birds, bird eggs, lichens, mushrooms, fungi

Sounds: faint bird-like calls during the night, young give high-pitched squeaks

Breeding: spring and summer mating; 40 days gestation

Young: 2–6 (average 3) offspring, 2 litters per year

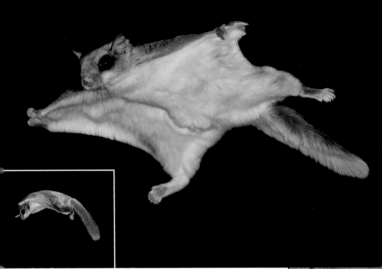

Signs: food has mysteriously disappeared from bird feeders overnight

Activity: nocturnal; active year-round, sometimes enters torpor during the very coldest parts of the winter

scat

Tracks: hind paw 1" (2.5 cm) long with 5 toes, forepaw ½" (1 cm) long with 4 toes; 1 set of 4 tracks; large landing mark (sitzmark) followed by bounding tracks, with hind paws falling in front of front prints; tracks lead to the base of a tree

Stan's Notes: The flying squirrel is the only nocturnal member of the Squirrel family in Texas. Its large bulging eyes enable it to see well at night. Common name "Flying Squirrel" is a misnomer because this animal does not have the capability to fly, only the ability to glide. In part, this is due to a large flap of skin (patagium) attached to its front and hind legs and sides of its body.

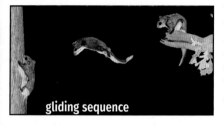
gliding sequence

To glide, a flying squirrel will climb to the top of a tree and launch itself, extending its four legs outward and stretching the patagium to make a flat, wing-like airfoil. Its flat tail adds some additional lift and acts like a rudder to help maneuver objects while gliding. Most glides are as long as 20–50 feet (6.1–15 m) and terminate at the trunk of another tree. To create an air brake for a soft landing, the squirrel will quickly lift its head and tuck its tail between its hind legs. After landing, it will scamper to the opposite side of the tree trunk, presumably to avoid any flying predators that may be following.

The flying squirrel is the most carnivorous of the tree squirrels, finding, killing, and eating small mice, dead flesh (carrion), and even baby birds and bird eggs. It is a gregarious animal, with many individuals living together in a nest.

Young are born helpless with eyes closed. Weaned at 5–7 weeks, they may stay with their mother through their first winter. Most flying squirrels live only 2–5 years, but some have lived as long as 10 years in captivity.

Spotted Ground Squirrel
Xerospermophilus spilosoma

Family: Squirrels (Sciuridae)

Size: L 5–8½" (13–21.5 cm); T 2–3½" (5–9 cm)

Weight: 3–5 oz. (85–142 g)

Description: Overall gray to brown with many faint whitish spots, more pronounced on the hind quarter of back. White-to-tan belly. Small round ears that don't stand erect. Short thin tail, covered with hair, often with a dark tip.

Origin/Age: native; 1–4 years

Compare: The Gray-footed Chipmunk (pg. 129) is smaller, has stripes on its body and face, and is restricted in range and elevation. Texas Antelope Squirrel (pg. 141) has a similar size, but lacks spots. The Mexican Ground Squirrel (pg. 149) is larger and has 9 rows of white spots.

Habitat: dry grasslands, sandy soils, grazed fields, desert scrub, low elevations below 5,000' (1,525 m)

Home: burrow, up to 20' (6.1 m) long, several feet deep, no excess dirt at the entrance, burrow system has many side tunnels and chambers and several entrances, main entrance is often under shrubs, chambers are lined with leaves and dried grass

Food: omnivore; mainly green plants; also eats seeds, lizards, baby mice, insects, and carrion

Sounds: high-pitched trill; will rapidly stomp its hind feet

Breeding: Apr–May mating; 27–28 days gestation

Young: 5–12 offspring 1–2 times per year; born naked with eyes closed, seen aboveground by about 4–5 weeks

Signs: small round entrance holes under shrubs, well-worn path to and from the burrow or to a secondary burrow

Activity: diurnal; active during midday with peak activity in late morning and late afternoon, usually seen running quickly back and forth to burrow, often standing upright in fields and meadows

Tracks: hind paw 1¼" (3 cm) long with 5 toes, forepaw ½" (1 cm) long with 4 toes; tracks usually seen around burrow entrance in dry sandy soils and dirt

Stan's Notes: An uncommon but widespread ground squirrel in Texas that is shy and secretive. Often unnoticed by the average observer. Usually associated with sparsely vegetated habitat such as desert scrub. Ranges from the southern edge of South Dakota to the eastern edge of Colorado, through most of New Mexico to western Texas, and west into northern and southeastern Arizona.

Prefers deep sandy soils with sparse vegetation and seems to be associated with silvery wormwood, a common shrubby plant. Less omnivorous than other ground squirrels, but still consumes a fair amount of insects, lizards, and any carrion it can find.

Males have larger home ranges than the females, from ¼–1 acre (0.1–0.4 ha). Maintains several burrows, which it excavates itself, often having a well-worn path on the ground between the burrows and 2–3 entrance holes at the base of a shrub. Lives in small groups with burrows spaced apart.

Breeding begins in mid-April and May, with young born about a month later and emerging from their burrow in July and August. Family groups often gather around the burrow entrance. When feeling threatened, individuals will stomp their feet before diving down the hole for safety.

One study showed that the aboveground activities of the Spotted Ground Squirrel typically are feeding and foraging (66 percent), altered behavior such as standing and looking about (15 percent), investigating (6 percent), and sunbathing, grooming, and other behaviors (8 percent). Active all year in areas of its range where winter is not severe.

Texas Antelope Squirrel
Ammospermophilus interpres

Family: Squirrels (Sciuridae)

Size: L 6–8" (15–20 cm); T 2–3½" (5–9 cm)

Weight: 3¾–5½ oz. (106–156 g)

Description: Overall reddish brown to gray with a white side stripe from shoulder to hip. Paler undersides. White ring around large dark eyes. Small short ears. Small bushy tail, dark gray with a grayish white underside and 2–3 black bands beneath.

Origin/Age: native; 1–5 years

Compare: Smaller than Mexican Ground Squirrel (pg. 149), which has many white spots and lacks the white lateral stripe. Similar size as the Spotted Ground Squirrel (pg. 137), which has small white spots on its back and sides.

Habitat: deserts and semideserts, creosote and juniper vegetation, dry rocky areas with hard packed soils, gravelly washes, low hills

Home: burrow, up to 10' (3 m) long, several feet deep, no excess dirt at the entrance, sometimes in rock crevices or other animal burrows, chamber lined with soft materials, has escape tunnels

Food: omnivore; green plants, seeds, stems of yucca, juniper, and several cactus species; insects

Sounds: usually silent, but gives a high-pitched alarm trill

Breeding: Feb–Apr mating; 30–35 days gestation

Young: 5–14 offspring once per year in April or May; born naked with eyes closed, independent after weaning, seen aboveground by about 5–6 weeks

Signs: small round entrance holes under shrubs, worn path to and from burrow; scat rarely seen

Activity: diurnal; most active in early morning and again in late afternoon, but can be seen during the middle of the day, usually seen running quickly back and forth to the burrow, becomes inactive during cold parts of winter

Tracks: hind paw 1½" (4 cm) long with 5 toes, forepaw ¾" (2 cm) long with 4 toes; tracks usually seen around burrow entrance in dry sandy soils and dirt

Stan's Notes: Inhabits the far western parts (Trans-Pecos area) of Texas in desert and low hilly regions. Prefers hard packed or gravelly soils and rocky slopes. Not commonly seen in flat sandy soils. Often associated with creosote and juniper vegetation.

Common name "Antelope" is for the flashy white underside of its tail, which is similar to that of a much larger mammal, the Pronghorn (pg. 331), also known as American Antelope. Runs very fast, like an antelope. Often flicks its tail when excited. A skilled climber, sometimes seen atop prickly pears and yuccas. Other times sits on top of large rocks, surveying the area.

Home range is up to 3 acres (1.2 ha), with daily travels covering less than half that area. Seldom sits still. Instead, it races around its territory, gathering food and nesting material and returning to its burrow. Feeds on green vegetation, seeds, insects, small lizards, and occasionally on smaller mammals. Digs its own burrow or takes residency in the burrow of other ground-dwelling species such as kangaroo rats or other ground squirrels.

Tolerates heat much better than cold and is often seen out during the hottest part of the day. Spreads out on the ground with its sparsely furred belly on the earth to cool itself. Also seeks shade during hot periods of the day for short periods before returning to normal activities.

Suns itself on rocks in winter. Retreats to its burrow during extremely cold weather and gains a layer of fat, but is thought not to hibernate.

Thirteen-lined Ground Squirrel
Ictidomys tridecemlineatus

Family: Squirrels (Sciuridae)

Size: L 6–8" (15–20 cm); T 2–5" (5–13 cm)

Weight: 4–9 oz. (113–255 g)

Description: Long, narrow brown body with 13 alternating tan and dark brown stripes from nape to base of tail. Small tan spots in the dark stripes. Short round ears. Large dark eyes. Short legs. Thin hairy tail, one-third the length of body.

Origin/Age: native; 1–3 years

Compare: Spotted Ground Squirrel (pg. 137) has a similar size and faint white spots. The pocket gophers (pp. 169–173) lack stripes and have very large front teeth and extremely long front claws.

Habitat: fields, pastures, grasslands, by roads, cemeteries

Home: burrow, up to 20' (6.1 m) long and often only several feet deep, with a hibernation chamber beneath the frost line and no excess dirt at the entrance, many side tunnels and several entrance and exit holes; will plug entrances and exits each night with plant material

Food: omnivore; green plants, seeds, insects, bird eggs, baby mice

Sounds: trill-like whistles when threatened or alarmed

Breeding: usually April mating; 27–28 days gestation

Young: 6–12 offspring once per year in May; born naked with eyes closed, becomes independent after it is weaned, seen aboveground by about 6 weeks

juveniles

Signs: small round entrance holes in grass, runways 2" (5 cm) wide worn in grass (made by its low-slung body and short legs) leading to and from the holes; scat is rarely seen since the animal often defecates in its burrow or in tall grass

Activity: diurnal; most active a couple of hours after sunrise and through midday, retires to its burrow 1–2 hours before sunset, does not come out on cold, windy or rainy days

Tracks: hind paw 1½" (4 cm) long with 5 toes, forepaw 1 (2.5 cm) long with 4 toes; tracks usually seen around burrow entrance

Stan's Notes: Not a gopher, but sometimes called Striped Gopher. Also called Federation Squirrel due to the pattern of stripes with spots on its body that resemble the US Stars and Stripes.

When there is frequent human contact at places such as roadside rest areas and golf courses, it can be friendly and is usually tame. Semisocial, interacting with other ground squirrels during the day when feeding. Individuals have separate burrows, but live in large colonies. Colonies are not highly organized and may result from a reduction in available habitat.

A fast runner, reaching speeds up to 8 mph (13 km/h). Zigzags and turns back when pursued. Stands upright to survey its territory. Gives a trill-like whistle at the first sign of danger and runs quickly to the main burrow or one of its short, dead-end escape burrows. Often stays inside the entrance, poking its head out, repeating its alarm call.

Stores some seeds in burrow for cold or rainy days. When insects are abundant, eats more insects than plants. Adds enough body fat in summer to start hibernating in September or October. Often enters hibernation sooner than chipmunks and emerges later, making it one of the longest true hibernators in Texas. Does not wake to feed, like chipmunks. Rolls up into a ball in the hibernation chamber. Heart rate, body temperature, and respiration drop dramatically. Reduced heart rate and respiration conserve energy in winter, but still loses up to half its body weight by spring.

Male emerges from hibernation before female. Mating occurs just after female emerges, usually in April. The short breeding season may explain why the female has only one litter each year. After mating, the male does not participate in raising young.

Young often do not disperse far and dig their own burrows near their mother. This substantially increases the colony size.

Mexican Ground Squirrel

Ictidomys mexicanus

Family: Squirrels (Sciuridae)

Size: L 7¾–9" (19.5–23 cm); T 4–6½" (10–16 cm)

Weight: 5–12 oz. (142–340 g)

Description: Long, narrow brown body with 9 rows of white spots on nape, back, and rump. Very short round ears that don't stand up above the head. Large dark eyes with white eye-rings. Short legs. Long hairy tail, three-quarters the length of body.

Origin/Age: native; 1–3 years

Compare: Texas Antelope Squirrel (pg. 141) lacks spots on its back and has white side stripes. Spotted Ground Squirrel (pg. 137) has less distinct white spots and a less furry tail. Thirteen-lined Ground Squirrel (pg. 145) has stripes and spots and is in eastern Texas. Consider range to help identify.

Habitat: fields, pastures, mesquite and creosote bushes, by roads, cemeteries, golf courses, city parks

Home: burrow, up to 20' (6.1 m) long, often several feet deep, no excess dirt at the entrance, many side tunnels, several entrances and exit holes, birthing chamber is often the deepest; will plug entrances and exits each night with plant material

Food: omnivore; green plants, seeds, insects, bird eggs, baby mice, carrion

Sounds: trill-like whistles when threatened or alarmed

Breeding: Mar–Apr mating; 28–30 days gestation

Young: 2–10 offspring once per year in May; born naked with eyes closed, becomes independent after weaning, seen aboveground by about 6 weeks

Signs: small round entrance holes in grass, runways 2" (5 cm) wide worn in grass or dirt (made by its low-slung body and short legs) leading to and from the holes; scat is rarely seen since the animal often defecates in its burrow or in tall grass

Activity: diurnal; most active a couple of hours after sunrise and through midday, retires to its burrow 1–2 hours before sunset, staying in on cold, windy, or rainy days; in central and western Texas it hibernates from November to March, but remains active in southern Texas year-round

Tracks: hind paw 1½" (4 cm) long with 5 toes, forepaw 1" (2.5 cm) long with 4 toes; tracks usually seen around burrow entrance

Stan's Notes: Occurs only in Texas, parts of southeastern New Mexico, and parts of Mexico. Seems to prefer sandy or gravelly soils. Common along highways, city parks, and golf courses, in many areas it is the most common ground squirrel.

Semisocial, interacting with other ground squirrels during the day when it feeds. Individuals have separate burrows, but live in large colonies. Colonies are not highly organized and may result from a reduction in available habitat. One squirrel may make use of several burrows nearby, with one as a main home and others for temporary shelter. The main burrow will have a birthing or brooding chamber lined with soft plant material.

Timid and shy, often standing upright to survey its territory. Gives a trill-like whistle at the first sign of danger and runs quickly to either the main burrow, a short secondary burrow, or one of its dead-end escape burrows. Often stays inside the entrance, poking its head out and repeating an alarm call.

Stores some seeds in its burrow for cold or rainy days. When insects are abundant, it eats more bugs than plants and is well known for feeding on dead animals on roads. In the northern part of the state it adds enough body fat during summer to hibernate in late November. Wakes often during winter on warm days to move about and can sometimes be seen aboveground. Rolls up into a ball in the hibernation chamber. Heart rate reduces and body temperature and respiration drop dramatically, which conserve its energy.

Male emerges from hibernation before the female. Mating occurs just after the female emerges, often in March. The short breeding season may explain why the female has only one litter each year. The male does not participate in raising young.

Young often do not disperse far and dig their own burrows near their mother. This substantially increases the colony size.

Rock Squirrel
Otospermophilus variegatus

Family: Squirrels (Sciuridae)

Size: L 11–13" (28–33 cm); T 6–8" (15–20 cm)

Weight: 1–2 lb. (0.5–0.9 kg)

Description: Long, narrow brown (sometimes brown-to-rust) body mottled with gray to tan. White ring around the eyes. Short round ears. Short legs. Long, thick bushy tail.

Origin/Age: native; 1–5 years

Compare: Eastern Gray Squirrel (pg. 157) lacks a mottled appearance and occurs in eastern Texas. Eastern Fox Squirrel (pg. 161) is larger than the Rock Squirrel and has a larger, bushier tail.

Habitat: rocky fields and hillsides, canyons, talus fields, shrublands, cliffs, along roads

Home: burrow, up to 20' (6.1 m) long and often only several feet deep, no excess dirt at the entrance, many side tunnels and several entrance and exit holes, chamber lined with leaves, dried grass, and especially tree bark stripped from the tree line

Food: omnivore; green plants, seeds, insects, fruit, nuts, bird eggs, baby mice, baby rabbits, carrion

Sounds: usually silent, but female gives a sharp clear whistle followed by a low-pitched trill when threatened or alarmed

Breeding: usually April mating; 27–28 days gestation

Young: 3–9 offspring once per year in April; born naked with eyes closed, becomes independent after it is weaned, seen aboveground by about 8–10 weeks

Signs: small round entrance holes under large rocks, worn path to and from the burrow; scat is rarely seen since the animal often defecates in its burrow or in dense vegetation

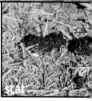

scat

Activity: diurnal; most active in early morning and again in late afternoon, can be seen during the middle of the day, sometimes seen sunning itself on large rocks, will become much less active during long hot spells, also becomes inactive during the colder parts of winter

Tracks: hind paw 2¼" (5.5 cm) long with 5 toes, forepaw 1½" (4 cm) long with 4 toes; tracks often seen near burrow entrance

Stan's Notes: A squirrel of rocky hillsides, canyons, talus fields, and dense vegetation. Can also be seen in shrublands and juniper woodlands in higher elevations. Increasingly found in urban and suburban areas that have large rocks or retaining walls. Occurs in west central Texas and is expanding its range in many places around the state.

An expert climber, often climbing trees and bushes to find nuts and fruit. Often confused with Eastern Gray Squirrel (pg. 157) when it is in trees. An opportunistic feeder, foraging on whatever is ripe or available at the time. Fills its large internal cheek pouches to help transport excess food back to the burrow for consumption. During the growing season, it prefers green plants and flowers. Also eats carrion, insects, and other protein when available. Has been known to catch, kill, and eat baby rabbits, nesting birds, or bird eggs.

Apparently does not store food in its burrow like other ground squirrels. Instead, it relies on accumulated fat for survival during bad weather. In colder parts of its range, it hibernates for short durations. Remains active all year in warmer parts of its range.

Usually colonial, with dominant males defending larger areas of territory during breeding season. Dominant females push out less dominant females and also subordinate males so they can be closer to dominant males during breeding season. Rock Squirrel densities are low, with only 5–6 individuals per acre. During the non-breeding season, adults occupy individual home ranges.

Only moderately social; adults don't interact with others outside of breeding season. Individuals familiar with each other approach one another head on and touch noses. Unfamiliar squirrels will approach each other at right angles with many threat displays.

Eastern Gray Squirrel
Sciurus carolinensis

Family: Squirrels (Sciuridae)

Size: L 9–10" (23–25 cm); T 8–9" (20–23 cm)

Weight: ¾–1½ lb. (0.3–0.7 kg)

Description: Overall gray or light brown fur with a white chest and belly. Large, bushy gray tail with silver-tipped hairs. Black morph is overall black with a reddish brown shine. Tail may also be reddish brown.

Origin/Age: native; 2–5 years

Compare: Smaller than the Eastern Fox Squirrel (pg. 161), which has a rusty orange tail.

Habitat: woodlands, suburban and urban yards, parks

Home: leaf nest (drey) in summer, hollow with a single entrance hole and lined with soft plant material, nest is in a tree cavity or old woodpecker hole in winter; male and female live in separate nests in summer, but together in winter

Food: omnivore; nuts, seeds, birdseed, fruit, corn, leaf buds, flowers, mushrooms, inner tree bark, baby birds, bird eggs, mice and other small mammals, insects, carrion

Sounds: hoarse, wheezy calls repeated many times when upset or threatened, chatters as an alarm call to warn of predators such as a house cat

Breeding: Jan–Feb mating; 40–45 days gestation

Young: 2–6 offspring once (sometimes twice) per year; born naked with eyes closed, eyes open at about 5 weeks, weaned at about 8–9 weeks, mother will push young away shortly after weaning

albino

black morph

scat

Signs: acorns and other large nuts split in half with the nutmeat missing, gnaw marks on tree branches stripped of bark, trees that lack new branches with green leaves in early summer

Activity: diurnal; active year-round, feeds late in morning and throughout the day, often rests a couple hours in the afternoon, may stay in nest for several days during very cold or hot periods

Tracks: hind paw 2¼" (5.5 cm) long with 5 toes, forepaw 1" (2.5 cm) long with 4 toes; 1 set of 4 tracks; forepaws fall side by side and behind hind prints

Stan's Notes: Common in eastern Texas. The black morph is born black and remains black. Pockets of black morph squirrels occur throughout the state. The albino morph, an entirely white squirrel with pink eyes, is more rare and does not live as long as the black morph.

Spends most of its life in trees, going to the ground only to feed on fallen nuts and seeds. Buries large amounts of nuts, most only ¼ inch (0.6 cm) underground. Studies show about 85 percent of these nuts are recovered. Nuts buried by scientists were recovered at a similar rate, indicating that squirrels find buried food by the sense of smell, not memory. Many squirrels "migrate" in years with poor nut crops, moving to find a new home range with an adequate food supply.

During the mating season, males will chase the females. Mating chases are long, with much jumping, bounding and biting.

Leaf nests (dreys) are located away from the main trunk of a tree and are constructed to shed water. A squirrel can have up to seven dreys, which are sometimes used as emergency nests. Usually born in a cavity nest, babies may be moved to a drey when the mother feels threatened. Mothers raise their young alone and move them from nest to nest, perhaps to avoid flea infestations. Studies show that 80 percent die in their first year due to predation by animals that eat squirrels such as coyotes, foxes, and hawks.

leaf nest

Considered a nuisance by many because it eats birdseed. Eats a variety of foods, however, including some mushrooms that are poisonous to people. Famous for its ability to access nearly any bird feeder, spending hours, days, or weeks devising a way to get the food. An industry has flourished around squirrel-proof feeders.

Eastern Fox Squirrel
Sciurus niger

Family: Squirrels (Sciuridae)

Size: L 10–15" (25–38 cm); T 8–13" (20–33 cm)

Weight: 1–2¼ lb. (0.5–1 kg)

Description: Dark gray fur with yellow and orange highlights. Bright rusty orange chin, chest, and belly. Large, fluffy, rusty orange tail. Very rare black morph has a white nose and belly and white-tipped ears.

Origin/Age: native; 2–5 years

Compare: The Eastern Gray Squirrel (pg. 157) is smaller and lacks a rusty orange tail.

Habitat: open woodlands, along rivers and streams, river valleys, suburban and urban yards, and parks

Home: leaf nest (drey) in summer, up to 24" (61 cm) wide, lined with soft plant material, usually with a side entrance, in a major fork near the main trunk of a tree, nest is in a tree cavity in winter and occupied by several individuals if enough food is available, also used for birthing; may build and use up to 6 nests

Food: omnivore; nuts, corn, pine cone seeds and other seeds, fruit, mushrooms, bird eggs, baby birds, mice, insects, carrion

Sounds: scolding calls similar to those of the Eastern Gray Squirrel, only more hoarse

Breeding: Jan–Feb and Jun–Jul mating; 40–45 days gestation

Young: 2–4 offspring 1–2 times per year; born with eyes closed, eyes open at about 30 days, leaves mother and on its own at about 3 months

black morph

Signs: large debris pile of split nutshells, whole corncobs, and husks strewn about underneath the feeding perch

Activity: diurnal; active year-round, usually begins feeding late in the morning, several hours after sunrise, often active during the middle of the day

Tracks: hind paw 2¾–3" (7–7.5 cm) long with 5 toes, forepaw 1½" (4 cm) long with 4 toes; 1 set of 4 tracks; forepaws fall side by side and behind hind prints

Stan's Notes: The largest of tree squirrels, with its bright rusty orange color making it easy to spot in the forest. Common name "Fox" was given for its oversized rusty orange tail, which is like that of the Red Fox. Some individuals are black with a white nose and belly and white-tipped ears, hence the species name *niger*.

Eastern Fox Squirrels spend more time farther away from trees than Eastern Gray Squirrels (pg. 157), searching for food on the ground and traveling, but both species collect, bury, and retrieve nuts in the same way, using their sense of smell to find buried

leaf nest

nuts. The Eastern Fox carries food back to its favorite spot to eat. Unlike the Gray, which uses nearly all available tree cavities for its nest, the Eastern Fox builds its large leaf nest in tree crotches.

It has a home range ten times larger than that of the Gray—up to 50 acres (20 ha)—so only several Eastern Fox Squirrels are found in any given area. In Texas it lives in a variety of forested habitats, mainly in open woodlands and along rivers and streams. Mostly seen in oak hickory woodlands that connect to other woodlands (green belt). In central Texas it is restricted to river valleys with nut-bearing trees. In western Texas most locate near river bottoms.

On examination of the stomach contents, it rarely has tapeworms or roundworms. One explanation is that the acorns it eats have large amounts of tannin, which is highly toxic to these parasites.

Several males "chase" one female prior to mating, following her throughout the day. Female will mate with more than one male.

Black-tailed Prairie Dog
Cynomys ludovicianus

Family: Squirrels (Sciuridae)

Size: L 12–14" (30–36 cm); T 3–4½" (7.5–11 cm)

Weight: 1½–3 lb. (0.7–1.4 kg)

Description: Uniform tan to light brown (sometimes cinnamon) with cream-to-white undersides. Short round ears that do not stand upright. Short, thin black-tipped tail, covered with short hairs.

Origin/Age: native; 1–4 years

Compare: Rock Squirrel (pg. 153) is smaller and has a large bushy tail. Eastern Fox Squirrel (pg. 161) is also smaller, with a bushy tail.

Habitat: grasslands, open fields, pastures

Home: extensive burrow systems, up to 30' (9.1 m) long and up to 7' (2.1 m) deep, large mounds of excess dirt at entrance, many side tunnels and chambers, several entrances, some burrows are intertwined with neighbor burrows, dried grass lines the nest chamber

Food: herbivore; grasses, sedges, roots

Sounds: variety of calls, high-pitched bark or alarm call given by several individuals, one after another

Breeding: Feb–Mar mating; 30–35 days gestation

Young: 4–8 offspring once per year; born naked with eyes closed, goes aboveground by about 4–7 weeks in May and June

pups

den entrance

barking

Signs: many large volcano-shaped domes with a single entrance hole, cut grass around the vicinity of the entrance

Activity: diurnal; active all day year-round, remains underground on extremely cold or rainy days, becomes inactive during the middle of the day in hot weather, becomes less active in winter

Tracks: hind paw 2–2½" (5–6 cm) long with 5 toes, forepaw 1" (2.5 cm) long with 4 toes; tracks usually seen around burrow entrance in dry sandy soils and dirt

Stan's Notes: Historically, about 98 percent of the prairie dogs in Texas were eliminated in favor of farming and raising livestock, thus their numbers are much lower than they once were. Their elimination, along with their land grooming habit of keeping out brush and maintaining grassland, is linked to the undesirable spread of brushland and the reduction of grassland, resulting in a detrimental effect on the livestock industry. Since cattle depend on grass for food, it would seem that, in hindsight, prairie dogs may be beneficial to the cattle industry after all.

The Black-tailed Prairie Dog occurs today in northwestern Texas, making its home in open fields and pastures. Lives in groups, creating towns that can be large and expansive, with hundreds of mounded entrance holes dotting the landscape.

Active during the day, spending most of its time aboveground, feeding on green plants. Does not hibernate, but will stay underground for several days during inclement weather.

A prairie dog has cones in its eyes, but no rods. As a result, it does not see very well in dim light or while underground.

Reproduces only once each year, with just 30 percent of young females reproducing in their first year. Young are born naked and eyes stay closed for 5 weeks. They are fully furred by 3 weeks and fully grown by autumn. Goes aboveground in late May and June.

At first, the young don't wander far from their burrow. Gradually, as they grow, they start to explore farther away in fields. Activities include playing, chasing, play fighting, wrestling, and running up to parents. Adults rarely exhibit these behaviors.

Adults mutually groom one another or touch noses, sniffing each other. An individual will stand erect at the entrance to its burrow and give a loud sharp bark at any sign of danger, throwing its head back while standing on hind legs. The bark is usually followed by other colony members echoing the call.

Plains Pocket Gopher
Geomys bursarius

Family: Pocket Gophers (Geomyidae)

Size: L 7–10" (18–25 cm); T 2–4" (5–10 cm)

Weight: 4½–12½ oz. (128–354 g)

Description: Light to dark brown upper body. Body widest at shoulders. Short legs. Pink feet. Extremely long front claws. Small round ears. Tiny eyes. Short naked tail.

Origin/Age: native; 2–5 years

Compare: Other gophers (pp. 172–173) are similar in size and shape. Range can be helpful in identifying these similar-looking critters. Look for the large front claws and short legs to help differentiate from any of the ground squirrels (pp. 137–153).

Habitat: loose sandy soils, fields, prairies, meadows, roadside ditches, golf courses, cemeteries, pastures

Home: network of tunnels, usually with 2 levels, some about 6" (15 cm) deep, used for gathering food, deeper tunnels down to 6' (1.8 m) are used for nesting and raising young

Food: herbivore; roots, bulbs, rhizomes

Sounds: inconsequential; rarely, if ever, heard

Breeding: spring mating; 50–55 days gestation

Young: 2–6 offspring once per year; born naked and helpless with eyes closed

tunneling

dirt mounds

claws

Signs: mounds of excess dirt as wide as 24" (61 cm) resulting from tunneling, ridges of dirt pushed up from tunneling; opening to tunnel system only rarely seen (would require digging into a dirt mound)

Activity: diurnal, nocturnal; active year-round, alternates several hours of activity with several hours of sleep

Tracks: forepaw ⅞" (2.3 cm) long, hind paw slightly smaller, both with well-defined claw marks; spends almost all of its time in its underground tunnel system, so tracks are rarely seen

Stan's Notes: There are 35 gopher species, all unique to North America. Ten of these occur in Texas and several are found only in the Lone Star State.

Specialized fur-lined cheek pouches or "pockets" give the pocket gopher its common name. Able to stuff large amounts of food or nesting material in its pouches, which extend from its cheeks to front shoulders. Cleans the pouches by turning them inside out.

Digs with its powerful front legs and long sharp claws, preferring loose sandy soils. Specialized lips close behind its large incisor teeth, keeping dirt out of the mouth while it digs. Incisor teeth are coated with enamel and grow throughout its life. Must gnaw on hard objects to keep its teeth sharp and prevent them from growing too large and rendering them useless. Sensitive hairs and bristles (vibrissae) on the wrists and tip of tail help it feel its way through tunnels. A narrow pelvis enables it to turn around while in tunnels. Its fur can lay forward or backward and allows the animal to back up without slowing down. Has a good sense of smell, but poor hearing and eyesight.

Lives entirely underground. Feeds on roots and bulbs of different plant species, depending upon the season and availability, and stores some food in underground chambers. Has been known to pull entire plants underground by the roots. Solitary except to mate, with only one animal living in a set of tunnels and mounds.

Has adapted well to human activity, often taking up residence in open grassy yards. This animal is very beneficial to the land since its digging aerates the soil, which allows for better drainage and nutrient mixing. However, it can be destructive to gardens and fields because it eats many of the plants.

Similar species on next page **171**

Additional Pocket Gopher Species

The word "gopher" is frequently used to describe a wide range of burrowing rodents that includes chipmunks and ground squirrels, but the term is properly restricted to pocket gophers, all of which have fur-lined cheek pouches on both sides of the mouth and large, powerful front feet and claws.

Pocket gophers can be difficult to distinguish, as they all share similar sizes, shapes and colors. Many have only chromosomal and biochemical differences, so consider range to help identify.

All nine other pocket gopher species in Texas have very limited ranges. Botta's Pocket Gopher is found along the western edge of the state. Baird's Pocket Gopher occurs in the eastern quarter of Texas. Yellow-faced Pocket Gopher, the second most abundant gopher in the state, ranges from the panhandle south through the Big Bend region and down the Rio Grande Valley to Brownsville. Jones's Pocket Gopher is seen in only a handful of counties at the bottom of the panhandle. The Strecker's Pocket Gopher occurs in fewer than ten counties in the central part of the state. Texas Pocket Gopher is found only in the southern tip of the state.

Botta's Pocket Gopher 5–7"

Baird's Pocket Gopher 5½–6½"

Yellow-faced Pocket Gopher 6–8¼"

Desert Pocket Gopher 7–7½"

Attwater's Pocket Gopher 7½–8½"

Llano Pocket Gopher 7–9½"

Jones's Pocket Gopher 8–8½"

Texas Pocket Gopher 8–8½"

Not pictured:
Strecker's Pocket Gopher 8–8½"

Desert Cottontail
Sylvilagus audubonii

Family: Rabbits and Hares (Leporidae)

Size: L 12–13½" (30–34.5 cm); T 1–2" (2.5–5 cm)

Weight: 1¾–3 lb. (0.8–1.4 kg)

Description: Overall gray to light brown with the center of the back darker than the sides. Longer black-tipped hairs, giving a grizzled appearance. Large hairless ears, longer than the length of head, with a black outside edge. Distinctive rusty red nape. Brown tail with a white cotton-like underside.

Origin/Age: native; 1–3 years

Compare: Since cottontails are so similar, range can help identify. The Eastern Cottontail (pg. 179) occurs throughout Texas. Swamp Rabbit (pg. 183) is the largest of cottontails and is found only in the eastern half of Texas.

Habitat: wide variety such as open fields, golf courses, brush or rock piles, along streams, shrublands, semideserts, deserts, creosote bushes

Home: shallow nest, lined with soft plant material and fur, covered with dry grasses and leaves

Food: herbivore; grass, dandelions, other green plants in spring and summer; twigs, bark, and other woody plants in winter

Sounds: loud high-pitched scream or squeal when caught by a predator such as a fox, coyote, or raptor

Breeding: year-round mating; 28 days gestation; starts to breed at 3 months

Young: 3–6 offspring 3–5 times per year; born naked and helpless with eyes closed

Signs: small woody twigs and branches near the ground are cleanly cut off and at an angle, while browse from deer and elk is higher up and has a ragged edge (due to lack of upper incisors in deer and elk); pea-sized, round, dry, woody, light brown pellets

scat

Activity: nocturnal, crepuscular; can also be seen during cooler days; often very active in late winter and early spring when males fight to breed with females

Tracks: hind paw 3–4" (7.5–10 cm) long, forepaw 1" (2.5 cm) long, small and round; 1 set of 4 tracks; forepaws fall one in front of the other behind hind prints

Stan's Notes: The most widespread of western cottontail species from Montana to Texas and west to California. Common name comes from the semidesert-like habitat where it is found and its cotton ball-like tail.

Usually freezes, hunkers down, and flattens ears if danger is near. Able to leap up to 12–15 feet (3.7–4.5 m) in a single bound while running, jumping sideways while running to break its scent trail. Can run as fast as 15 mph (24 km/h) for a short distance, which enables it to elude some predators. Uses a well-worn set of trails in winter, usually under thick cover of bushes. When flushed, it runs quickly in a zigzag pattern, circling back to its starting spot. On hot, lazy summer days, it will stretch out in shady areas to cool itself.

Males often remain in a small area of only 10–15 acres (4–6 ha), while females reside in areas about half that size. Usually not a territorial animal, but fights will break out among males during mating season. Interspersed with chasing, males face each other, kick with front feet, and jump high into the air.

After mating, the female excavates a small area for a nest, lines it with soft plants and fur from her chest for comfort, and camouflages the entrance. Mothers nurse their babies at dawn and dusk, but may stay away for up to a day at a time. Once the young open their eyes and are moving around outside the nest, they are on their own and no longer receive help from their mother.

A successful rabbit species, with females usually breeding before they reach 1 year of age and some producing up to 35 offspring annually. Most of the cottontail young, however, do not live any longer than a year.

Eastern Cottontail
Sylvilagus floridanus

Family: Rabbits and Hares (Leporidae)

Size: L 14–18" (36–45 cm); T 1–2" (2.5–5 cm)

Weight: 2–4 lb. (0.9–1.8 kg)

Description: Overall gray to light brown. Black-tipped hairs give it a grizzled appearance. Usually has a small white (rarely black) spot on forehead between the ears. Large pointed ears, rarely with a black outside edge. Distinctive rusty red nape. Brown tail with a white cotton-like underside.

Origin/Age: native; 1–3 years

Compare: Since cottontails are so similar, use range to help identify. Desert Cottontail (pg. 175) is smaller and is found mainly in the western half of Texas. Swamp Rabbit (pg. 183), the largest cottontail, is not seen in the western half of Texas.

Habitat: wide variety such as open fields, brush piles, rock piles, along rivers and streams, woodlands

Home: shallow nest, lined with soft plant material and fur, covered with dry grasses and leaves

Food: herbivore; grass, dandelions, other green plants in spring and summer; saplings, twigs, bark, and other woody plants in winter

Sounds: loud high-pitched scream or squeal when caught by a predator such as a fox or coyote

Breeding: late Feb–Mar mating; 30 days gestation; starts to breed at 3 months

Young: 3–6 offspring up to 5 times per year; born naked and helpless with eyes closed

camouflaged

scat

Signs: small woody twigs and branches near the ground are cleanly cut off and at an angle, while browse from deer is higher up and has a ragged edge (due to the lack of upper incisors in deer), bark is stripped off of saplings and shrubs; dry, pea-sized light brown pellets, round and woody; soft green pellets are ingested and rarely seen

Activity: nocturnal, crepuscular; often very active during late winter and early spring when males fight to breed with females

Tracks: hind paw 3–4" (7.5–10 cm) long, forepaw 1" (2.5 cm) long, small and round; 1 set of 4 tracks; forepaws fall one in front of the other behind hind prints

Stan's Notes: The most widespread of the eight cottontail species in North America, seen in the eastern United States, all of Texas, and most of Mexico. Transplanted to many areas that historically did not have cottontails. Common name was given for its cotton ball-like tail.

Usually stays in a small area of only a couple acres. Often freezes, hunkers down and flattens ears if danger is near. Quickly runs in a zigzag pattern, circling back to its starting spot when flushed. Able to leap up to 12–15 feet (3.7–4.5 m) in a single bound while running. Also jumps sideways while running to break its scent trail. Uses a set of well-worn trails in winter, usually in thick cover of bushes. Cools itself on hot summer days by stretching out in shaded grassy areas.

Usually not a territorial animal, with fights among males breaking out only during mating season. Interspersed with chasing, males face each other, kick with front feet, and jump high into the air.

After mating, the female excavates a small area for a nest, lines it with soft plants and fur from her chest for comfort, and camouflages the entrance.
Mothers nurse their helpless babies at dawn, as well as at dusk. Once the young can open their eyes and are moving outside the nest,

cooling

they are on their own and get no further help from their mother. One of the most reproductively successful rabbit species in North America, with some females producing as many as 35 offspring annually; however, most young do not live longer than 1 year.

Like other rabbits and hares, this species produces fecal pellets that are dry and brown or soft and green. Eats the green pellets to regain the nutrition that wasn't digested initially.

Swamp Rabbit
Sylvilagus acquaticus

Family: Rabbits and Hares (Leporidae)

Size: L 18–22" (45–56 cm); T 1–2" (2.5–5 cm)

Weight: 3½–5 lb. (1.6–2.3 kg)

Description: Short hair (pelage), overall dark brown, with the center of back darker than the sides. Gray underneath. Short broad ears, sparsely haired. Orange eye-ring. Feet and nape of neck rusty red. Brown tail with a white cotton-like underside.

Origin/Age: native; 1–3 years

Compare: Since cottontails are so similar, range can help identify. The Swamp Rabbit is the largest of the cottontails and occurs in the eastern half of the state. The Eastern Cottontail (pg. 179) is smaller, lacks rusty red feet and is found across Texas. Desert Cottontail (pg. 175) lives in the western half of the state.

Habitat: river bottoms, coastal marshes, just about any other place with standing water

Home: shallow nest, lined with soft plant material and fur, covered with dry grasses and leaves, under a fallen log, at the base of a tree

Food: herbivore; grass, other green plants

Sounds: loud high-pitched scream or squeal when caught by a predator such as a fox, coyote, or raptor

Breeding: Jan–Sep mating; 38–40 days gestation; starts to breed during the first year

Young: 2–4 offspring 2–3 times per year; born furred, with eyes and ears closed, but these open within days

Signs: small woody twigs and branches near the ground are cleanly cut off and at an angle; pea-sized, round, dry, woody, light brown pellets placed on logs and stumps or other high places

Activity: nocturnal, crepuscular; can also be seen during the day, often very active during February and March when males fight to breed with females

Tracks: hind paw 4–5" (10–13 cm) long, forepaw ½" (2.5 cm) long, small and round; 1 set of 4 tracks; forepaws fall one in front of the other behind hind prints

Stan's Notes: The largest of the cottontails and true to its name, living in wet ditches, coastal marshes, swamps, and along rivers and streams. Truly a semiaquatic rabbit that will take to the water when pursued. Will swim not only to avoid predators, but also to get where it wants to go. An excellent swimmer, often completely submerging except for its nostrils. This ability is not seen in other species of rabbits.

Feeds on terrestrial and aquatic green plants, and woody plants. Along the coast it lives in cane thickets, which gives rise to a local name, Cane Cutter, for its habit of eating cane. Usually very secretive during the day and only seen when flushed from its hiding place. Often leaves fecal pellets on stumps, downed logs, or other high and dry places.

More territorial than other rabbit species. One rabbit has a home range of 7 acres (2.8 ha), usually having mainly wetlands, which it refuses to leave even when chased by a predator. It will double back or circle around to find a thick stand of thorny shrubs in which to hide. Also uses underground burrows for escape. One of the only rabbit species in which the males mark territory with scent from a gland on the chin.

Nest (form) is a depression in the ground lined with moss and rabbit fur, usually at the base of a fence post or large tree. Swamp Rabbit gestation is longer than in other rabbit species, resulting in the young being born fully furred, with eyes and ears opening within days. Young are able to walk within days of their birth.

Numbers of these rabbits have been decreasing due to wetland draining and wetland forest clearing. Habitat fragmentation has also been a major problem, isolating populations and reducing breeding opportunities.

Black-tailed Jackrabbit
Lepus californicus

Family: Rabbits and Hares (Leporidae)

Size: L 18–24" (45–61 cm); T 2–3" (5–7.5 cm)

Weight: 4–8 lb. (1.8–3.6 kg)

Description: Gray to light brown in summer with black-tipped hair, giving it a grizzled appearance. Light white belly. Extremely long ears with black tips. Long legs. Large hind feet. Large brown eyes. A large, puffy white tail with black on top, extending to the rump. All white in winter (some individuals have brown patches) with black-tipped ears.

Origin/Age: native; 1–5 years

Compare: This hare stands much taller than the cottontails (pp. 175–183) and is as tall as a medium-sized domestic dog. Its huge size and large ears make it easy to identify.

Habitat: semideserts, deserts, scrublands, grasslands, mountains, elevations from sea level up to 8,000' (2,440 m)

Home: shallow nest under sagebrush and other shrubs or beneath logs, lined with dry grasses and hair from the mother, uses a burrow in winter

Food: herbivore; green plants in summer; twigs, bark, leaf buds, dried grasses, and berries in winter

Sounds: inconsequential; may give a loud, shrill scream when captured by a large predator

Breeding: Feb–May mating; 30–40 days gestation

Young: 1–11 offspring; 4–5 times per year; born fully furred with eyes open and incisor teeth erupted, able to move around within an hour of birth

Signs: trails worn between feeding areas and resting sites; hard, dry, woody, slightly flattened, dark brown pellets, ½" (1 cm) wide, or moist green pellets

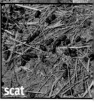
scat

Activity: mostly nocturnal, crepuscular; can be seen during cloudy or overcast days

Tracks: hind paw 4–5½" (10–14 cm) long and 2" (5 cm) wide, forepaw 1" (2.5 cm) long, small and round; 1 set of 4 tracks; forepaws are slightly offset side by side or fall one in front of the other behind hind prints

Stan's Notes: The most abundant jackrabbit species across most of the western states including throughout Texas. Sometimes called Jackass Rabbit, although it is actually a type of hare. Hard to mis-identify because it is so large and runs with a seesaw-like rocking from front to hind feet. Black on tail and rump is best seen when it runs. Can leap as far as 20 feet (6.1 m) and run up to 45 mph (72 km/h) for a short distance, slowing to a series of low leaps from 4–10 feet (1.2–3 m).

The enormous ears have a generous blood flow, which dissipates heat during summer. The ears also provide an excellent means of predator detection. The large hind legs facilitate high jumps and quick escapes from predators and are used for defense, kicking and scratching with its claws. Does not like water, but is a good swimmer and may plunge into water to escape a predator.

Usually solitary, but may be seen in large groups, especially in spring when it gathers for mating. Females can be slightly larger than males (bucks), but there are no obvious differences between sexes. When bucks fight, they kick with hind feet and bite.

Rests under logs or other shelter (shade) during the day and will flush only if contact is very close. During winter it snuggles in bur-rows that may be connected by tunnels, resting with its large ears pressed flat against its back.

Female constructs a simple nest—a shallow depression lined with grasses and fur plucked from her chest. Babies can run within an hour of their birth. They are eating plants at 2 weeks and weaned shortly after, fully independent at 4 weeks. If born early enough in the season, young females can breed before their first winter.

Reingestion of soft fecal pellets (coprophagy) occurs in hares, as it does in rabbits.

Long-tailed Weasel
Mustela frenata

Family: Weasels and Skunks (Mustelidae)

Size: L 8–16" (20–40 cm); T 3–6" (7.5–15 cm)

Weight: 3–9 oz. (85–255 g)

Description: Light brown in summer with a long black-tipped brown tail, brown feet and white-to-yellow chin, throat, chest, and belly. Long tubular body. Short legs. White in the winter with a black-tipped tail. Male slightly larger than female.

Origin/Age: native; 5–10 years

Compare: Much smaller than Black-footed Ferret (pg. 199), which doesn't turn white in winter and is always associated with prairie dogs.

Habitat: woods, forest edges, fields, grasslands, farms, wet areas, rocky deserts

Home: nest made from grass and fur, usually in an old chipmunk, ground squirrel, or mole burrow or beneath logs and rocks; often has several nests in its territory

Food: carnivore, insectivore; small to medium mammals such as mice, voles, chipmunks, squirrels, and rabbits; will also eat small birds, bird eggs, carrion, and insects

Sounds: single loud trills or rapid trills, squeals

Breeding: summer (Jul–Aug) mating; 30–34 days gestation; ova develop for 8 days after fertilization, then cease development, implantation is delayed up to 8–10 months after mating

Young: 4–8 offspring once per year from April to June

Southwestern

Signs: long, thin, often dark scat with a pointed end, contains hair and bones, often on a log or rock, very similar to mink scat

Activity: primarily nocturnal, diurnal mostly during the winter; hunts during the day for several hours, then rests and sleeps for several hours

Tracks: hind paw ¾–1" (2–2.5 cm) long, forepaw slightly smaller, both round with well-defined nail marks, 5 toes on all feet; 1 set of 4 tracks when bounding; 12–20" (30–50 cm) stride

Stan's Notes: This is a very active predator that runs in a series of bounds with back arched and tail elevated. A good swimmer and will climb trees to pursue squirrels. Quickly locates prey using its excellent eyesight and sense of smell, dashes to grab it, then kills it with several bites to the base of the skull. Favorite foods include mice and voles. Sometimes hunts for larger prey such as rabbits. Eats its fill and caches the rest. Consumes 25–40 percent of its own body weight in food daily.

winter

Uses scents and sounds to communicate with other weasels. Deposits scat on rocks and trails to mark territory. Both sexes apply an odoriferous, oily substance from their anal glands onto rocks, trees, and other prominent landmarks to communicate territory, social status, sex, and willingness to mate. The odor is rarely detectable by people, especially after a few days. Male territory is 25–55 acres (10–22 ha). Female territory is smaller. Defends the territory against other weasels.

Solitary except during mating season and when a mother is with her young. Constructs nest in an abandoned animal burrow or beneath logs and rocks, using grass for nesting material along with the fur of small animals it has eaten.

In Texas and across the southern range some individuals may not change to white in winter. The Southwestern, a variety in Texas and southwestern states, has a dark face, forehead and ears, with a white patch between the eyes and in front of the ears.

Mink
Mustela vison

Family: Weasels and Skunks (Mustelidae)

Size: L 14–20" (36–50 cm); T 6–8" (15–20 cm)

Weight: 1½–3½ lb. (0.7–1.6 kg)

Description: Dark brown to nearly black or brown to blond, often with a luster. Short, round dark ears. Small white patch on the chin. Long tubular body with short legs. A long bushy tail, darker near the tip. Male slightly larger than female.

Origin/Age: native; 5–10 years

Compare: Larger than Long-tailed Weasel (pg. 191), which is lighter brown with white-to-yellow underside. Mink does not turn white in winter.

Habitat: along rivers, lakes, and streams; wetlands, farms, forests

Home: burrow, entrance is 4" (10 cm) wide

Food: carnivore; small to medium mammals such as voles, mice, chipmunks, rabbits, and squirrels, but favors muskrats; also eats small birds, bird eggs, snakes, frogs, toads, crayfish, and fish

Sounds: chatters, scolds, hisses, snarls when alarmed or fighting other minks

Breeding: Jan–Apr mating; 32–51 days gestation; implantation delayed, length of delay is dependent upon when the female mates during the season

Young: 3–6 offspring once per year; born covered with fine hair and eyes closed, eyes open at about 7 weeks, weaned at 8–9 weeks, mature at 5 months

brown morph

Signs: small, thin dark scat, usually pointed at one end, usually containing bone, fur, and fish scales, deposited on rocks and logs along lakes and rivers

scat

Activity: nocturnal, diurnal; hunts for several hours, then rests several hours

Tracks: hind paw 2–3¼" (5–8 cm) long with 5 toes, forepaw 1¼–1¾" (3–4.5 cm) long with 5 toes, both round with well-defined nail marks; 1 set of 4 tracks when bounding; 12–25" (30–64 cm) stride; tracks may end at the edge of water

Stan's Notes: Also known as the American Mink. This is the most aquatic of weasels, usually seen along banks of rivers and lakes across the eastern half of Texas. Its thick, oily, waterproof fur provides great insulation and enables the animal to swim in nearly freezing water. Its partially webbed toes aid in swimming. Can swim underwater as far as 100 feet (30 m) before surfacing. Able to dive down to 15 feet (4.6 m) for its favorite food, muskrats.

Hunts on land for chipmunks, rabbits, snakes, and frogs. Moves in a series of loping bounds with its back arched and tail held out slightly above horizontal. When frightened or excited, releases an odorous substance from glands near the base of its tail.

Burrow is almost always near water, often under a tree root or in a riverbank. May use a hollow log or muskrat burrow after killing and eating the occupants. Active burrows will often have a strong odor near the entrance. Most burrows are temporary since minks are almost constantly on the move looking for their next meal.

The male maintains a territory of up to 40 acres (16 ha), with the female territory less than half the size. Will mark its territory by applying a pungent discharge on prominent rocks and logs. It is a polygamous breeder.

The pelt of a mink is considered to be one of the most luxurious. Demand for the fur has led to the establishment of mink ranches, where the fur color can be controlled by selective breeding.

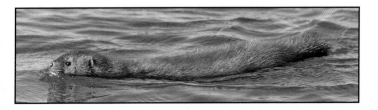

Black-footed Ferret
Mustela nigripes

Family: Weasels and Skunks (Mustelidae)

Size: L 15½–19" (39–48 cm); T 4–5½" (10–14 cm)

Weight: 1½–2¼ lb. (0.7–1 kg)

Description: Body is tan to yellowish brown with a dark stripe down the center of back. Black mask around eyes. Elongated tubular body with short legs. Black legs and feet. Light-colored tail with a black tip.

Origin/Age: native; 5–10 years

Compare: Larger than Long-tailed Weasel (pg. 191), which lacks the black mask, legs and feet of the Ferret.

Habitat: grasslands, fields, prairie dog towns

Home: takes over a prairie dog burrow or ground squirrel tunnel; home range of 20–50 acres (8–20 ha) or more

Food: carnivore; mainly prairie dogs; also eats ground squirrels, rabbits, reptiles, and some insects

Sounds: much growling and snarling when cornered

Breeding: winter (Feb–Mar) mating; 42–45 days gestation; no delayed implantation

Young: 3–5 offspring once per year in April or May; first appears aboveground in July, when it is about three-quarters the size of an adult

Signs: narrow piles of freshly excavated dirt at the entrance of a burrow; long, thin, often dark scat with a pointed end, contains hair and bones, very similar to mink scat

Activity: primarily nocturnal, diurnal only during winter when adults are looking for mates and moving from burrow to burrow during the day; most active between one and four o'clock in the morning during the rest of the year, hunts mainly at night until it catches something, then rests for up to 6 days, feeding on its kill

Tracks: hind paw 2–2¾" (5–7 cm) long, forepaw slightly smaller, both round with well-defined nail marks, 5 toes on all feet; 1 set of 4 tracks when bounding; 12–20" (30–50 cm) stride

Stan's Notes: The least known of all weasels in North America. Was listed as an endangered species prior to being declared extinct in 1979, when the last ferret died in a zoo. No wild ferrets were known to exist, but in 1981, a ranch dog in Meeteetse, Wyoming, brought home the body of a Black-footed Ferret, which led to the discovery of a small wild population. By 1985 the wild population was struck with a fatal disease, killing all but 18 individuals. These few remaining ferrets were trapped and then bred in captivity. The ferrets were reintroduced back into the wild in several states including Wyoming and Arizona starting in 1991. Last seen in the Lone Star State in 1953 and again in 1963. Many would like to see this animal reintroduced into Texas.

Black-footed Ferrets have coevolved with prairie dogs and are so closely linked, you can't find ferrets without a prairie dog town. Ferrets use prairie dog burrows for their homes and hunt and eat prairie dogs for food. A ferret might expand the burrow or add chambers and will often leave the burrow and take up residency in another one as it searches for food.

Ferrets live alone in burrows and will come together only during mating or when females have young. Young leave their mothers at the end of their first summer and are sexually mature at 1 year of age. Will start to breed right away and may live up to 10 years in the wild. Extremely nocturnal, only coming aboveground well after dark, and usually back in the burrow well before daylight.

Very susceptible to canine distemper, resulting in many ferret deaths. Also suffers from plague. Highly impacted by poisoning programs designed to control prairie dogs.

Prospects for the survival of the Black-footed Ferret are good as long as the prairie dog population stays healthy and the habitat and prey remain intact.

American Badger

Taxidea taxus

Family: Weasels and Skunks (Mustelidae)

Size: L 20–30" (50–76 cm); T 3–6" (7.5–15 cm)

Weight: 8–25 lb. (3.6–11.3 kg)

Description: Coarse, grizzled gray upper and yellowish brown underside. A dark snout with a distinctive white stripe from the nose upward, between the eyes, and to the nape. White cheeks and ears. Large wide body. Short powerful legs with long, sharp nonretractable (nonretractile) nails on front feet. Small gray tail. Male larger than female.

Origin/Age: native; 3–10 years

Compare: Look for American Badger's unique body shape, short legs, and the white stripe between the eyes.

Habitat: along roads, fields, grasslands, woodland edges

Home: large den, often in a road embankment or grassy hillside, digs its own, may overtake and enlarge a prairie dog burrow; uses den for birthing, raising young, and during torpor

Food: carnivore, insectivore; small mammals such as voles, mice, chipmunks, rabbits, and ground squirrels; also eats small birds, bird eggs, snakes, frogs, toads, and insects

Sounds: loud snarls and growls

Breeding: Jul–Aug mating; 30–40 days gestation; implantation delayed until February after mating

Young: 1–5 offspring once per year in March or April; born covered with fine fur and eyes closed, eyes open at about 4 weeks, weaned at about 8 weeks

den entrance

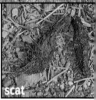

scat

Signs: large pile of unearthed dirt in front of den entrance, can be seen from a great distance, bones, uneaten body parts and scat frequently scattered near the den entrance; long thin scat, segmented, often dark, contains hair and bones

Activity: nocturnal; usually does not leave den until well after dark to hunt for small mammals, occasionally leaves den during the day

Tracks: forepaw and hind paw 2" (5 cm) long and wide, round with narrow pad, separate nail marks, 5 distinct toes on all feet; fore and hind prints fall near each other when walking, 6–12" (15–30 cm) stride

Stan's Notes: The least weasel-like of weasels. Uniquely shaped, its wide flattened body, short powerful legs, and narrow snout make it well suited to burrow and live underground. Has second eyelids (nictitating membranes), which protect its eyes while it digs. Uses its long, sharp front claws to dig through coarse rocky soil, expelling dirt between its hind legs like a dog. Can dig fast enough to catch ground squirrels while they are in their burrows. Has an excellent sense of smell. Believed to be able to determine just by the scent of a burrow whether or not it is occupied.

Secretive and avoids contact with people. Has the reputation of being aggressive, especially a mother defending her young. Very vocal when threatened, snarling and growling loudly.

Hunts cooperatively with coyotes. While a badger excavates one tunnel entrance, a coyote will wait for the occupant to emerge at an auxiliary escape tunnel. Frequently the coyote will chase the occupant back down the burrow to the waiting badger.

It is not a true hibernator, but enters a condition called torpor that resembles hibernation, during which the body temperature falls approximately 10°F (–12°C) and heart rate and respiration decrease to approximately half the normal rate. Torpor lasts only 20–30 hours at a time. Badgers remain awake for up to 24 hours between periods of torpor, during which time body temperature and heart rate return to normal. Because of this energy-saving torpor cycle, the body rarely uses up its stored fat by spring.

Male has a large home range, where several females also may live. Lacks a family structure. Male stays solitary while female raises young on her own. Young stay with the mother until their first autumn, when they are fully grown and can hunt on their own.

Northern River Otter
Lontra canadensis

Family: Weasels and Skunks (Mustelidae)

Size: L 2½–3½' (76–107 cm); T 11–20" (28–50 cm)

Weight: 10–30 lb. (4.5–13.5 kg)

Description: Overall dark brown-to-black fur, especially when wet, with a lighter brown-to-gray belly. Silver-to-gray chin and throat. Small ears and eyes. Short snout with white whiskers. Elongated body with a long thick tail, tapered at the tip. Male slightly larger than female.

Origin/Age: native; 7–20 years

Compare: Much larger than the Muskrat (pg. 109), which has a long, thin naked tail. The American Beaver (pg. 117) has a wide flat tail.

Habitat: rivers, streams, medium to large lakes

Home: permanent and temporary dens

Food: carnivore, insectivore; fish, crayfish, frogs, small mammals, aquatic insects

Sounds: loud shrill cries when threatened, during play will grunt, growl, and snort, chuckles when with mate or siblings

Breeding: Mar–Apr mating; 200–270 days gestation; implantation delayed for an unknown amount of time, entire reproduction process may take up to a year, female mates again days after giving birth

Young: 1–6 offspring once per year in March or April; born fully furred with eyes closed, eyes open at around 30 days, weaned at about 3 months

sleeping

Signs: haul outs, slides, and rolling areas; scat is dark brown to green, short segments frequently contain fish bones and scales or crayfish parts, deposited on lakeshores, riverbanks, rocks, or logs in water

scat

Activity: diurnal, nocturnal; active year-round, spends most of time in water, comes onto land to rest and sleep, curls up like a house cat to sleep

Tracks: hind paw 3½" (9 cm), forepaw slightly smaller, both round with a well-defined heel pad and toes spread evenly apart, 5 toes on all feet; 1 set of 4 tracks when bounding; 12–24" (30–61 cm) stride

Stan's Notes: A large semiaquatic animal once seen in the eastern half of Texas in major rivers, but greatly reduced by hunting and trapping. Now limited to suitable habitat in far eastern Texas only. Protected in the Lone Star State.

Well suited to life in water, with a streamlined body, webbed toes, long guard hairs and dense oily undercoat. Special valves close the nostrils underwater, enabling submersion for up to 6–8 minutes.

A playful, social animal, not often very afraid of people. Can be seen in small groups (mostly mothers with young), swimming and fishing in rivers and lakes. Frequently raises its head high while treading water to survey surroundings. Enjoys sliding on its belly down well-worn areas of mud or grass (slides) along riverbanks or lakeshores just for fun. Can dive to depths of 50 feet (15 m). Sensitive to water pollution, quickly leaving a contaminated area.

Often feeds on slow-moving fish that are easy to catch such as catfish and suckers. Mistakenly blamed for eating too many game fish. Comes to the surface to eat, bringing larger items to eat at the shore. Uses its forepaws to manipulate, carry, and tear apart food. Creates haul outs, well-worn trails leading from the water that often end up being littered with fish heads, scat, and crayfish parts.

Likes to roll, which flattens areas of vegetation up to 6 feet (1.8 m) wide. Rolling areas have a musky odor from scent marking and usually contain some scat. Very vocal, giving a variety of sounds, such as a loud whistle, to communicate over long distances.

Male defends territory against other males. Female moves freely in and out of male territory. Digs den in a riverbank or lakeshore, often with an underwater entrance. May use an old beaver lodge. Has permanent and temporary dens. Permanent den, lined with leaves, grasses, mosses, and hair, usually is where young are born.

Becomes sexually mature at 2–3 years. A male is generally solitary except during mating season and not around for the birth of the young. Returns in midsummer to help raise them.

Western Spotted Skunk
Spilogale gracilis

Family: Skunks (Mephitidae)

Size: L 12–14" (30–36 cm); T 4½–7" (11–18 cm)

Weight: 1–1½ lb. (0.5–0.7 kg)

Description: White spot on head between eyes. Several stripes along the back and sides, some horizontal, some vertical, others broken up into dashes and spots. Black tail with a large white tip.

Origin/Age: native; 2–5 years

Compare: The Eastern Spotted Skunk (pg. 219) is slightly larger, with a smaller white tip on its tail. Striped Skunk (pg. 227) is larger and lacks the white spot between the eyes and white-tipped black tail.

Habitat: oak woodlands, canyons with rivers, woodland edges, shrublands, semideserts, mountainsides, suburban and urban areas

Home: no regular burrow, mainly a rock crevice, hollow log or tree crevice, under a deck or porch

Food: omnivore; insects, spiders, small mammals, earthworms, grubs, bird eggs, amphibians, corn, fruit, berries, nuts, seeds, reptiles

Sounds: generally quiet; will stomp front feet and exhale in a loud "pfittt," also chatters its teeth

Breeding: Sep–Oct mating; 30–33 weeks gestation; implantation delayed until 20–30 days after mating

Young: 2–6 offspring once per year in April or May; born naked with black and white skin (matching the color of its future fur coat) and eyes closed, musky odor at 8–10 days, eyes open at about 30 days

Signs: pungent odor, more obvious when the skunk has sprayed, can be detected even if it has not sprayed; small, dark, segmented cylindrical scat, deposited on trails and at the entrance to den

Activity: mostly nocturnal; more active in summer than winter

Tracks: hind paw 1½" (4 cm) long with 5 toes and a well-defined heel pad, appearing flat-footed, forepaw 1" (2.5 cm) long and wide with 5 toes; 1 set of 4 tracks when bounding; fore and hind prints are very close together, 3–5" (7.5–13 cm) stride

Stan's Notes: It was reported in the early 1900s that this species was more common than the Striped Skunk (pg. 227) in its range. Occurs throughout the southwestern quarter of Texas, but not common in any area today, with populations fluctuating widely. For reasons unknown, populations of Western Spotted Skunk and the very similar Eastern Spotted Skunk (pg. 219) have decreased dramatically across the country. For a time, Western and Eastern Spotted Skunks were considered one species. The Western is the smaller species and has a larger white tip on its tail.

The smallest of the skunks and also the most weasel-like in body shape and behavior. Fast, agile and adept at climbing trees. An expert mouser that, like a house cat, is good at controlling small mammal populations around ranches. Sometimes called Civet Cat, but this name is misleading because it is neither a civet (mongoose, member of the Viverridae family), nor is it a cat. Considered by some people to have the softest fur of all animals.

Much more carnivorous than the Striped Skunk. Constantly on the move, looking for its next meal. Strictly nocturnal, extremely secretive, and rarely seen.

When threatened it rushes forward, stomps its feet, and stands on its forepaws with hind end elevated. Agile enough to spray from this position. Able to spray as far as 10 feet (3 m) with surprising accuracy. Odor is similar to that of the Striped Skunk.

Breeds in autumn unlike other skunk species, which are spring breeders. Young are born in April and May. Young females are breeding at 4–5 months, which means they are mating by their first fall. Solitary except for breeding or when mothers have young.

Hooded Skunk
Mephitis macroura

Family: Skunks (Mephitidae)

Size: L 12–15" (30–38 cm); T 12–20" (30–50 cm)

Weight: 2–4 lb. (0.9–1.8 kg)

Description: A small skunk with several stripe patterns. Bushy tail, equal to body length or longer, all white, all black, or black with a white tip. Thin white stripe between ears and eyes. Upper neck has longer hair (ruff), like a hood. Male larger than female.

Origin/Age: native; 2–5 years

Compare: Striped Skunk (pg. 227) is much larger, with a tail shorter than the length of its body. The Hog-nosed Skunk (pg. 223) has long front claws and a pig-like naked snout. Western Spotted Skunk (pg. 211) is smaller, with a white spot between its eyes, not a stripe.

Habitat: rocky canyons, desert scrub, woodland edges, streams

Home: burrow, often in a hollow log or tree crevice, rock crevice, brush pile, or small rock pile in summer

Food: omnivore; insects, worms, grubs, mammals, bird eggs, amphibians, reptiles, corn, fruit, nuts, seeds

Sounds: generally quiet; will stomp front feet and exhale in a loud "pfittt," also chatters its teeth

Breeding: Feb–Mar mating; 60–61 days gestation; implantation presumed delayed up to 2 weeks after mating

Young: 3–8 offspring once per year; born naked with black and white skin (matching the color of its future fur coat) and eyes closed, musky odor at 8–10 days, eyes open at about 24 days

Signs: pungent odor, more obvious when the skunk has sprayed, detectable even when it has not sprayed; segmented cylindrical scat, often dark, deposited on trails and at the entrance to the den

Activity: mostly nocturnal; more active in summer than winter

Tracks: hind paw 2–2¾" (5–7 cm) long with 5 toes and a well-defined heel pad, looking flat-footed, forepaw 1–1¾" (2.5–4.5 cm) long and wide with 5 toes; alternating fore and hind prints are very close together when walking, 4–6" (10–15 cm) stride

Stan's Notes: This species is also known as White-sided Skunk, Southern Skunk, or Zorrillo. Its range runs from Central America into North America, extending throughout Mexico and reaching into the United States, where it is found only in western Texas, southwestern New Mexico, and the southern half of Arizona.

The fur of Hooded Skunk is longer and softer than other skunk species. Long hairs at the base of its head make the animal appear like it is wearing a hood and are the reason for its common name.

This skunk has several stripe patterns. The single stripe pattern is mostly white with one wide white stripe from the back of the head going down the back and extending throughout the tail (shown). The double stripe form has a thin white stripe from the front legs to the hind quarters and a larger central white stripe running down the back from head to tail. A third form has an all-black body with only thin lateral stripes and black tail with a small white tip.

Often misidentified or confused with the Striped Skunk (pg. 227) in Texas because the two have very similar stripe patterns. Best to look at tail length and presence of the hood to help identify.

More nocturnal than other skunk species and also less aggressive when trapped or cornered. Often seen dead at roadsides where it was too slow to move out of the way of passing vehicles. Has the same odor as other skunks and is very closely related to both the Striped Skunk and Hog-nosed Skunk (pg. 223).

Feeds primarily on insects and consumes more plant material, such as cactus fruit and berries, than the other skunk species. It is the least studied of the skunks, which has caused its natural history information to be limited.

Eastern Spotted Skunk
Spilogale putorius

Family: Skunks (Mephitidae)

Size: L 13–15" (33–38 cm); T 3–8" (7.5–20 cm)

Weight: 1½–2 lb. (0.7–0.9 kg)

Description: White spot on the head between the eyes. About 6 white stripes along the back and sides, some broken into dashes and spots. Black tail with a white tip.

Origin/Age: native; 2–5 years

Compare: Western Spotted Skunk (pg. 211) has a larger white-tipped black tail and occurs in a different range. Striped Skunk (pg. 227) is much larger, lacks spots, and has fewer stripes.

Habitat: mixed woodlands, woodland edges, farmlands, river bottoms, suburban neighborhoods, rocky canyons, desert scrub

Home: no regular burrow, may use a hollow log or old woodchuck den, area under a deck or porch in summer, digs its own burrow, mostly for winter use; female uses burrow only to give birth

Food: omnivore; voles, mice, and other small animals; insects; also eats earthworms, grubs, corn, nuts, berries, seeds, and amphibians

Sounds: generally quiet; will stomp front feet and chatter its teeth

Breeding: Feb–Mar mating; 50–65 days gestation; implantation delayed until 2 weeks after mating

Young: 1–6 offspring once per year; born covered in fine black and white fur with eyes and ears closed, eyes and ears open at about 30 days

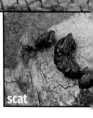

scat

Signs: pungent odor, worse when the animal has sprayed, can be detected even if it has not sprayed; small dark scat, often with a pointed end, deposited on trails and logs

Activity: nocturnal, diurnal; spends the day in a hollow log, brush pile, haystack or wall of a barn or similar building, forages for food mostly on the ground at night

Tracks: hind paw 1¼" (3 cm) long with 5 toes, forepaw 1" (2.5 cm) long with 5 toes, both tracks round with several separate toe and heel pads; 1 set of 4 tracks when bounding; fore and hind prints are very close together, 3–5" (7.5–13 cm) stride

Stan's Notes: Once common in Texas, in most areas this small skunk is now rare. Because one of its main foods is insects, it is thought the widespread use of insecticides is responsible for this dramatic decline.

Considered by some to have the finest, softest fur in the animal world. A semisocial animal, but secretive. Fast, agile, and adept at climbing trees. An expert mouser that, like a house cat, is good at controlling small mammal and insect populations around farms. Constantly on the move, looking for its next meal. Much more carnivorous than the Striped Skunk (pg. 227).

Also called Civet Cat, but this is a misleading name because it is neither a civet (mongoose, member of the Viverridae family), nor is it a cat. Species name *putorius* is Latin and refers to the pungent smell of its spray.

When threatened, it rushes forward, stomps its feet and stands on its forepaws with hind end elevated. Agile enough to spray from this position. Can spray up to 10 feet (3 m) with surprising accuracy. Odor is similar to that of the Striped Skunk.

Female matures sexually at 9–11 months. Mother raises the young without any help from the male.

Hog-nosed Skunk
Conepatus leuconotus

Family: Skunks (Mephitidae)

Size: L 14–16" (36–40 cm); T 7–16" (18–40 cm)

Weight: 3–6 lb. (1.4–2.7 kg)

Description: A large skunk with a simple, sharply bicolored pattern, black on the bottom, white on the top. Long naked snout. Short powerful legs with long downward curving front claws. Lacks any white stripe or mark between eyes. All-white tail, same length as the body or shorter.

Origin/Age: native; 2–5 years

Compare: Unique-looking skunk that is easily identified by its solid white tail and back, and black face, sides, and legs. Look for the long naked nose and long curved front claws to help identify.

Habitat: rocky canyons, rocky slopes, foothills, mesquite grasslands, brushlands

Home: rock crevice or hollow, occasionally in a brush pile, especially in summer

Food: omnivore; mainly insects, spiders, grubs, small mammals, fruit

Sounds: generally quiet; will stomp front feet and exhale in a loud "pfittt," also chatters its teeth

Breeding: Feb–Mar mating; 59–61 days gestation; implantation presumed delayed until 2 weeks after mating

Young: 2–4 offspring once per year; born naked with black and white skin (matching the color of its future fur coat) and eyes closed, musky odor at 1–2 days

Signs: pungent odor, more obvious when the skunk has sprayed, detectable even when it has not sprayed; segmented cylindrical scat, often dark, deposited on trails and at the entrance to the den

Activity: mostly nocturnal; can be active during the day in winter when the days are warm and nights are very cold

Tracks: hind paw 2¼–3¼" (5.5–8 cm) long with 5 toes and a well-defined heel pad, looking flat-footed, forepaw 1–1¾" (2.5–4.5 cm) long and wide with 5 toes and distinct claw marks; alternating fore and hind prints are very close together when walking, 4–6" (10–15 cm) stride

Stan's Notes: The only skunk with an elongated naked nose and long curved front claws. Uses its claws and powerful front legs to dig up insects, which are the mainstay of its diet. This rooting behavior has given it another common name, Rooter Skunk. When actively hunting it turns soil over like a plow, leaving freshly exposed soil in its wake. Spends a lot of time in rock piles and other rocky areas where it roots around for food. Will feed on other small mammals if it can catch them.

Can be very tolerant of people, but if approach is too close it will defend itself in usual skunk-like fashion, which consists of rushing forward, stomping its feet, and raising its tail just before spraying.

Usually nocturnal, it can be seen hunting during the day in midwinter. Often avoids hot desert areas. Not very common in any part of its range. Range was once as far north as Oklahoma, but this skunk apparently isn't adapting well to habitat change. Now found only in the southern two-thirds of Texas, Arizona, and southern New Mexico, extending down into Mexico. Populations have been declining dramatically all across its range, especially in the Lone Star State.

Once considered to be two individual species. Based on genetic analysis, now viewed as a single species called by several other common names such as Common Hog-nosed Skunk and White-backed Hog-nosed Skunk.

Two varieties occur in Texas. These are known as Western Hog-nosed Skunk and Eastern Hog-nosed Skunk. The Western (shown) is found in western Texas, Arizona, New Mexico and most of Mexico. It has a broad stripe running from the top of its head to the base of its tail, which is long, bushy, and white. The Eastern (not shown) lives in southern Texas and eastern Mexico. The Eastern has a thin wedge-shaped stripe that gets very narrow to nonexistent on the rump, with a white tail.

Striped Skunk
Mephitis mephitis

Family: Skunks (Mephitidae)

Size: L 20–24" (50–61 cm); T 7–14" (18–36 cm)

Weight: 6–12 lb. (2.7–5.4 kg)

Description: Variable stripe patterns. Black with a large white stripe from ears to tail, sometimes splitting down the hind quarters. Large bushy tail, shorter or equal to body length, white or black with white sides. Thin white stripe down the center of head between ears and eyes. Male larger than female.

Origin/Age: native; 2–5 years

Compare: Hooded Skunk (pg. 215) has longer hair on its upper neck (ruff) and a longer tail than its body. Western Spotted Skunk (pg. 211) is smaller, with a white spot between its eyes, not a stripe.

Habitat: woodlands, river bottoms, fields, suburban and urban areas, mountains, rocky canyons, outcrops

Home: burrow, often in hollow log or tree crevice, under a deck, porch, firewood, or rock pile in summer

Food: omnivore; insects, spiders, small mammals, earthworms, grubs, bird eggs, amphibians, corn, fruit, berries, nuts, seeds, reptiles

Sounds: generally quiet; will stomp front feet and exhale in a loud "pfittt," also chatters its teeth

Breeding: Feb–Apr mating; 62–66 days gestation; implantation delayed until 18–20 days after mating

Young: 4–7 offspring once per year; born naked with black and white skin (matching the color of its future fur coat) and eyes closed, musky odor at 8–10 days, eyes open at about 24 days

spraying

scat

Signs: pungent odor, more obvious when the skunk has sprayed, can be detected even when it has not sprayed; segmented cylindrical scat, often dark, deposited on trails and at entrance to the den

Activity: mostly nocturnal; more active during summer than winter

Tracks: hind paw 2–3½" (5–9 cm) long with 5 toes and a well-defined heel pad, appearing flat-footed, forepaw 1–1¾" (2.5–4.5 cm) long and wide with 5 toes; alternating fore and hind prints are very close together when walking, 4–6" (10–15 cm) stride

Stan's Notes: This animal is found across the United States and well into Canada. While it can be highly variable in color and pattern across this large range, in Texas it has three unique stripe patterns. One has a large white stripe running from its ears to the tail, sometimes splitting down the hind quarters, with white on the sides of its tail (shown). Another has two narrow stripes from the head to the rump. Others have two narrow stripes from the top of the head to the shoulders, with a mostly black body and white edges on the tail. Tail length is shorter or about the same length as its body, unlike the Hooded Skunk (pg. 215), which has a longer tail than its body.

Bred in the early 1900s for its fur, which explains the wide variety of colors in pet skunks today. The white stripes of a skunk, which vary in length and width from one animal to another, can be used to identify individuals. Some have such wide stripes that they appear to be all white, although most are not albino.

The prominent black and white markings warn predators that it should not be approached. Will face a predator when threatened, arch its back, and raise its tail while chattering its teeth. If this does not deter the predator, it will rush forward, stomp its feet, stand on forepaws with tail elevated, and spray an oily, odorous yellow substance from glands at the base of its tail near the anus.

Able to spray 5–6 times up to 15 feet (4.6 m) with surprising accuracy. This substance can cause temporary blindness and intense pain if it enters the eyes. Holding the animal by its tail off the ground will not prevent it from spraying. Genus and species names refer to the spray and mean "bad odor."

This is a solitary, secretive skunk that wanders around in a slow, shuffling waddle in search of food. Does not hibernate, but will hole up in its burrow for a few weeks to two months during cold weather. Known to burrow in groups of up to 15 individuals, often all females. This can be a problem when the burrow is under a house because of the cumulative smell.

Ringtail
Bassariscus astutus

Family: Raccoons (Procyonidae)

Size: L 12–15½" (30–39 cm); T 12–16" (30–40 cm)

Weight: 2–2½ lb. (0.9–1.1 kg)

Description: Cat-like in shape. Overall yellowish gray with long dark guard hairs, giving it a grizzled appearance. Small head with large pointed ears, like a fox. Very large dark eyes with a white ring around each eye. Large tail with 7–8 black and white or brown and white rings and a black tip.

Origin/Age: native; 6–10 years

Compare: Smaller and thinner than the Northern Raccoon (pg. 235), which has a distinctive black mask and shorter tail. Much smaller than White-nosed Coati (pg. 239), which has smaller eyes and ears and much less distinct rings on tail.

Habitat: canyonlands, semideserts, scrublands, brushlands, rocky areas

Home: hollow tree, rock crevices, or underground den where trees are absent, den is lined with grasses and leaves

Food: omnivore; crayfish, fish, reptiles, amphibians, nuts, fruit, green leaves, suet, bird eggs, insects, small mammals such as mice, ground squirrels, and baby birds

Sounds: snarls, growls, and barks as alarm and threat calls

Breeding: Feb–Jun mating; 54–65 days gestation; female in heat (estrus) for only 3–6 days

Young: 1–5 offspring once per year, often in May or June; born with eyes closed, leaves den at 7–8 weeks

Signs: elongated cylindrical scat of various sizes and shapes, often placed in just one place, creating large common latrines that are used to mark territories

Activity: nocturnal; active year-round except during cold snaps in winter

Tracks: hind paw 2¼–3" (5.5–7.5 cm) long with 5 long toes and no claw marks, forepaw 1½–2" (4–5 cm) long, slightly longer than wide with 5 distinct toes and no claw marks; tracks rarely seen because of the rocky habitat

Stan's Notes: A unique animal in Texas that has a body like a cat, face and ears like a fox, a tail like a raccoon, and climbs like a squirrel. An excellent mouser, once captured to control rodent populations in mines and referred to as Miner's Cat. Also known as Ringtail Cat, Civet Cat, or Rock Cat. Another common name, Cacomistle, coming from the Mexican Nahuatl People, translates to "half mountain lion."

This animal is an excellent climber, with sharp claws that facilitate climbing trees and large rocks. The hind feet rotate 180 degrees, allowing it to climb down trees and rocks like a squirrel, face first. Can also jump across great distances, similar to squirrels.

A nocturnal critter, active only in the middle of the night. Rarely seen during the day. An expert hunter, bringing down a wide variety of mice, ground squirrels, woodrats, and other small mammals, along with lizards and large insects. Pounces on prey and kills it, biting the base of the neck, and eats meals headfirst.

Common in the Trans-Pecos area and Edwards Plateau of western and central Texas. Much less common in the forested regions of eastern Texas. Recent studies found it to be more widespread and possibly more common than previously noted.

Individuals have a large home range. A male occupies 108 acres (43 ha), while females cover 50 acres (20 ha). Home ranges of the males do not overlap. Some ringtails hunt and travel together where ranges overlap. Social structure is otherwise unknown.

Males mark their territories with urine. Anal glands in both sexes emit a foul odor when the animal is threatened or alarmed.

Northern Raccoon
Procyon lotor

Family: Raccoons (Procyonidae)

Size: L 24–25" (61–64 cm); T 7–16" (18–40 cm)

Weight: 12–35 lb. (5.4–15.8 kg)

Description: Overall gray to brown, sometimes nearly black to silver. Distinctive black band across face (mask), eyes and down to the chin. White snout. Bushy, black-tipped brown tail with 4–6 evenly spaced dark bands or rings.

Origin/Age: native; 6–10 years

Compare: Very distinctive animal. The black mask and dark rings on the tail make it hard to confuse with any other species.

Habitat: almost all habitats, rural and urban, always near water

Home: hollow tree, or underground den where trees are absent

Food: omnivore; crayfish, fish, reptiles, amphibians, nuts, fruit, green leaves, suet, birdseed (especially black-oil sunflower seeds and thistle), small mammals, baby birds, bird eggs, insects

Sounds: very loud snarls, growls, hisses, and screams are common (and may be frightening) during the mating season, soft purring sounds and quiet chuckles between mothers and babies

Breeding: Feb–Jun mating; 54–65 days gestation; female in heat (estrus) for only 3–6 days

Young: 3–6 offspring per year, usually in May; born with eyes closed, leaves den at 7–8 weeks

Signs: pile of half-digested berries deposited on a log, rock, under a bird feeder, or on top of a garbage can; scat is usually cylindrical, 2" (5 cm) long and ¾" (2 cm) wide, but can be highly variable due to diet

scat

Activity: nocturnal; active year-round except during cold snaps in winter

Tracks: hind paw 3½–4½" (9–11 cm) long with 5 long toes and claw marks, forepaw 2½–3" (6–7.5 cm) long, slightly longer than wide with 5 distinct toes and claw marks; forepaws land (register) next to hind prints, 8–20" (20–50 cm) stride

Stan's Notes: Raccoons are native only to the Americas from Central America to the United States and lower Canada. Northern Raccoon is found throughout Texas in nearly all habitats. Common name is from the Algonquian word *arougbcoune*, meaning "he scratches with his hands." Known for the ability to open such objects as doors, coolers, and latches. Uses its nimble fingers to feel around the edges of ponds, rivers, and lakes for crayfish and frogs. Known to occasionally wash its food before eating, hence the species name *lotor*, meaning "washer." However, it is not washing its food, but kneading and tearing it apart. The water helps it feel the parts that are edible and those that are not. A strong swimmer.

juveniles

Able to climb any tree very quickly and can come down headfirst or tail end first. Its nails can grip bark no matter which way it climbs because it can rotate its hind feet nearly 180 degrees so that the hind toes always point up the tree.

Active at night, sleeping in hollow trees or other dens during the day. Often mistakenly associated with forests. Also lives in grasslands, using underground dens, but never is far from water.

Usually solitary as an adult. Does not hibernate but may sleep or simply hole up in a comfortable den in January and February, depending on the weather. Will occasionally den in small groups of the same sex, usually males, or females without young.

Males wander many miles in search of a mate. Females use the same den for several months while raising their young, but move out afterward and find a new place to sleep each night. Males are not involved in raising young. Young remain with the adult female for nearly a year.

White-nosed Coati
Nasua narica

Family: Raccoons (Procyonidae)

Size: L 25–30" (64–76 cm); T 15–27" (38–69 cm)

Weight: 10–25 lb. (4.5–11.3 kg)

Description: Overall light to dark brown, frequently cinnamon, sometimes with a lighter saddle-like shape on the back. Distinctive black marks on face with white around eyes and a white snout. Short round ears. Short legs with white on upper part of front legs. Long curved claws. A very long, bushy tail with faint rings, tapering to a point at the end. Often holds tail up straight or bent like a question mark.

Origin/Age: native; 6–10 years

Compare: Northern Raccoon (pg. 235) has a black mask and shorter tail with rings on it. Ringtail (pg. 231) is much smaller, with a bushier, dark-ringed tail.

Habitat: mountain forests, wooded canyons, near water

Home: no real home or den, spends the night in trees, daytime on the ground; uses a maternity den in a rock outcrop for birthing

Food: omnivore; fruit, nuts, large insects, amphibians, reptiles, small mammals, baby birds, bird eggs

Sounds: very loud growls and snarls, hisses and whimpers, soft chattering and chirps

Breeding: Jan–Mar mating; 75–77 days gestation

Young: 4–6 offspring once per year, in spring; born with eyes closed, leaves the den at 5–6 weeks, young have darker coats than adults, young males stay with the troop until 2 years of age

sleeping

Signs: pile of half-digested berries deposited on a log or rock; scat is usually cylindrical, 2" (5 cm) long and ¾" (2 cm) wide, but can be highly variable depending on diet

Activity: diurnal; active year-round, sleeps in trees at night

Tracks: hind paw 3–3½" (7.5–9 cm) long with 5 long toes and claw marks, forepaw 2–2½" (5–6 cm) long with 5 distinct toes and very long claw marks; forepaws land (register) behind the hind prints, 7–15" (18–38 cm) stride

Stan's Notes: Considered a threatened species in Texas. A very interesting relative to the more common and well-known raccoon. Also known as Antoon, Coatimundi, or just Coati (pronounced "ko-WHA-tee"). Often called Tejon ("badger") in Mexico. All members of the Raccoons family live in the New World. The coati is found in Mexico and Central America, with small populations living in southern Texas and Arizona. Isolated populations seen in southern California and Florida may be the South American Coati (*N. nasua*) (not shown), a different species with a dark snout and distinct rings on its tail. Probably introduced.

Active during the day, foraging for food in large groups. A group, or troop, consists of up to 50 females and young, but smaller sizes are more common. Males are solitary except for a few weeks during breeding season when they seek receptive females.

Feeds by rooting around in leaf litter for insects, nuts, and berries. Climbs trees for fruit and often returns repeatedly until all fruit is gone. A true omnivore, eating whatever food it finds. Feeds in the morning and late in the evening, lowering its tail when feeding.

An excellent climber, using its long tail to help balance on small branches. Travels holding its tail upright. Swims well. Naps and grooms during the day, especially when it is hot.

Sleeps in trees at night to avoid predators. Active all year and does not use a den except when giving birth. Females will use the den with their young for the first 5–6 weeks until the young are strong enough to keep up with the troop.

More gregarious than other members of the Raccoons family and much more vocal. Young play noisily, while adults are most vocal when interacting with each other. Spends time grooming itself and other individuals while giving soft soothing sounds.

Like the raccoon, the coati tolerates people well and will raid camps, garbage cans, and parking lots for anything edible. Highly intelligent and able to problem solve and remember tasks.

Nine-banded Armadillo
Dasypus novemcinctus

Family: Armadillos, Sloths, and Anteaters (Dasypodidae)

Size: L 15–21" (38–53 cm); T 9–14" (23–36 cm)

Weight: 8–17 lb. (3.6–7.7 kg)

Description: Unique-looking round body covered in 9 heavy bony plates (armor). Each scale looks like it is comprised of small scales. Tan to brown, usually covered in mud, but can be shiny. Long, narrow pointed snout. Tiny eyes and tall oval ears. Short legs. Long nails. Long narrow tail, lacking hair.

Origin/Age: native; 4–7 years

Compare: Hard to confuse with any other animal. Opossum (pg. 251) has a furred body. Look for segmented body armor and a hairless tail to help identify.

Habitat: grasslands, open woodlands, scrublands, wetlands

Home: burrow, several entrances with little excavated dirt, sometimes at the base of a rock, usually in a small hill or riverbank, up to 15' (4.5 m) long and 3' (1 m) deep, 1 chamber lined with vegetation

Food: omnivore; mainly insects; also eats the carrion of rabbits, squirrels, snakes, lizards, and frogs

Sounds: sniffing noises, several grunts and groans

Breeding: Jul–Aug mating; 115–120 days gestation; implantation delayed until late October or November

Young: up to 6 offspring once per year; born with eyes open and shell intact (although not hardened), young often genetically identical, with 4 (quadruplets) the most common number produced from a single fertilized egg, weaned at about 3 months

tail

Signs: burrow entrance that is 6–8" (15–20 cm) wide; round gray pellets, ¾" (2 cm) wide, resembling clay marbles due to the amount of soil consumed while digging up insects

Activity: diurnal, nocturnal; can be seen at many times of the day and night, does not come out on cold, rainy days

Tracks: hind paw 2" (5 cm) long with 5 toes, forepaw 1½–1¾" (4–4.5 cm) long, with 4 toes; 1 set of 4 tracks; hind paws fall slightly behind fore prints; tracks often in a straight line, 4–6" (10–15 cm) stride with a partial tail drag mark, seen in dry dirt and mud along streams and wetlands

Stan's Notes: Member of an order of animals with unique backbone joints that allow them to bend more than animals that have backbones without special joints. Animals in this group are seen only in the New World, in South, Central, and North America. While there are several armadillo species, only the Nine-banded is found in North America. Expanding its range in the United States, having moved up from Mexico. Has been introduced into Arkansas, Florida, and other areas of the country.

Needs to drink water each day and is limited in Texas by the lack of freestanding water. A dramatic decline in Texas populations over the past 20 years has reduced the likelihood of seeing this interesting critter.

Gets the common name "Nine" from the number of armored, jointed (articulated) plates on its body. Able to curl up into a tight ball, with the plate on top of its head protecting the joint where the front and back of the armored shell meet. When threatened, the first defense of an armadillo is to run off or hide in its burrow, where it lodges itself, using its armor as protection. Armored up inside a burrow makes it nearly impossible to pull the animal out. If the burrow is not near, it will roll up into an impenetrable ball.

Eyesight is not that great, so sometimes it stands upright to sniff the air for danger, supporting itself with its tail. Spends most of its time out of the burrow with its nose to the ground, sniffing for insects or other food. An excellent excavator, digging under fallen logs or tearing apart logs, using its short, thick, powerful legs and long toe nails to burrow and search out food. A desirable animal to have around due to the large number of insects it consumes at ranches and farms.

Young can walk within hours of birth. Appearing like miniature piglets, they follow their mother around in a line, single file.

North American Porcupine
Erethizon dorsatum

Family: Porcupine (Erethizontidae)

Size: L 20–26" (50–66 cm); T 6–12" (15–30 cm)

Weight: 7–30 lb. (3.2–13.5 kg)

Description: A short, stocky body with short legs, an arching back and quills on rump and tail. Dark brown to nearly black. Longest guard hairs are often white-tipped. Ears are small, round and barely visible. Tiny dark eyes. Small feet with long claws.

Origin/Age: native; 5–10 years

Compare: Similar size as Striped Skunk (pg. 227), but lacks white stripes. Look for the obvious body shape (arching back) and large white-tipped quills to identify. Can be seen on the ground or in trees.

Habitat: coniferous and deciduous forests, grasslands, rocky slopes

Home: den in a large hollow tree or a fallen hollow log, underground burrow

Food: herbivore; soft bark, inner bark of conifers, green plants, tree leaves, leaf buds

Sounds: much vocalization with loud, shrill screeching during mating, mothers make soft grunts and groans to communicate with their babies

Breeding: Oct–Nov mating; 7 months gestation; female is receptive to mating (estrus) for only 8–12 hours; has a very long gestation period for a rodent

Young: 1 offspring once per year in May or June; born fully quilled with teeth erupted and eyes open, feeds itself within 1 week, weaned by 1 month, stays with mother until the first autumn

scat

juvenile

Signs: large pieces of bark gnawed from coniferous trunks, tooth marks on exposed wood, cleanly chewed twigs and branches laying nearby, chew marks on buildings, canoe paddles, and ax handles; pile of pellets, often irregular in size and shape due to diet, may have soft segmented scat in summer, hard individual pellets in winter

Activity: mostly nocturnal, crepuscular; active year-round

Tracks: hind paw 3–3½" (7.5–9 cm) long, wide oval with claw marks and dotted (stippled) impression from rough, pebbled pads, forepaw 2–2½" (5–6 cm) long, oval with claw marks; 1 set of 2 tracks; fore and hind prints alternate left and right with toes pointing inward, hind paws fall near or onto fore prints, tail drag mark between each set of prints in mud

Stan's Notes: A slow, solitary animal that is usually seen sleeping at the top of a tree or slowly crossing a road. Makes up for its slow speed by protecting itself with long, barb-tipped guard hairs that are solid at the tip and base and hollow in between. It has over 30,000 sharp quills, which actually are modified hairs loosely attached to a sheet of muscles just beneath the skin. Unable to throw the quills, but will swing and hit with its tail, driving the tail quills deep into even the toughest flesh. Some report that quill barbs are heat sensitive and open when entering flesh, making them very hard to extract. Quills provide such an excellent defense, only few predators are capable of killing a porcupine.

Uses a den in a large tree for sleeping during the day or for holing up for several days or weeks during cold snaps in winter. Feeds on inner bark of coniferous trees in winter, but moves to the ground to eat green vegetation in spring and summer.

Males find females during the mating season by sniffing the base of trees and rocks where a female might have passed. Males can become very aggressive toward other males, often fighting during the breeding season.

Elaborate mating with much vocalization and several males often attending one female. When the female is ready to mate, she will raise her tail to permit typical mounting.

Babies have an atypical birth, emerging headfirst with eyes open, teeth erupted, and body covered with soft, flexible quills. Quills dry and become stiff within a couple hours.

gray morph

Virginia Opossum
Didelphis virginiana

Family: Opossums (Didelphidae)

Size: L 25–30" (64–76 cm); T 10–20" (25–50 cm)

Weight: 4–14 lb. (1.8–6.3 kg)

Description: Two color morphs, gray and dark. Gray-to-brown body, sometimes nearly black. White head, throat, and belly. Long narrow snout with a pink nose. Wide mouth. Oval, naked black ears. Long, scaly, naked, semiprehensile pinkish tail. Short legs and 5 pink toes on the feet. First toe on each hind foot is thumb-like and lacks a nail.

Origin/Age: native; 3–5 years

Compare: Muskrat (pg. 109) is much smaller, all brown and rarely far from water. Norway Rat (pg. 99) also has a long naked tail, but Virginia Opossum is larger with large dark ears and a pink nose. Norway Rat is rarely seen in trees.

Habitat: deciduous forests, farmlands, yards, grasslands, wetlands, along streams and rivers, cities

Home: leaf nest in an underground den or hollow log

Food: omnivore; insects, sunflower and thistle seeds, nuts, berries, fruit, leaves, bird eggs, fish, reptiles, amphibians, small mammals, road kill, worms

Sounds: low growls, hisses and shows teeth if threatened, soft clicks between mothers and young

Breeding: Jan–Feb mating; 8–14 days gestation

Young: 2–13 (usually 5–6) offspring once per year; newborns the size of a navy bean crawl to mother's external fur-lined pouch, where they attach to a nipple for as long as 2 months

in pouch

dark morph

dark morph

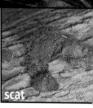

scat

Signs: overturned garbage cans; scat on ground under sunflower seed and Nyjer thistle feeders

Activity: nocturnal; can be seen during the day in winter

Tracks: hind paw 2" (5 cm) long with 5 toes, large thumb-like first toe points inward and lacks a nail, forepaw 1½" (4 cm) long with 5 toes spread out; fore and hind prints are parallel, 7" (18 cm) stride, often has a tail drag mark

Stan's Notes: The regular gray morph is found in the northern three-quarters of the state. A dark, nearly black variety that has a black mask and black feet occurs in southern Texas.

The only marsupial found north of Mexico. A unique-looking, interesting animal, the size of a house cat. It has 50 teeth, more than any other mammal in the state. Usually solitary, moving around on the ground from place to place. Also climbs trees well, using its tail to aid in climbing, holding onto branches (semiprehensile). An adult opossum cannot hang by the tail like a monkey, but the young seem able to, perhaps due to their lighter weight.

Frequently feeds on dead animals along roads and is often hit by vehicles. Not a fast mover, it will hiss if threatened and show its short, pointy teeth. When that doesn't work, it often will roll over and feign death with eyes closed, mouth open, and tongue hanging out, "playing 'possum." Does not hibernate, but sleeps in dens for weeks during the coldest part of winter.

playing 'possum

Males give loud, aggressive displays during the breeding season and will scent-mark by licking themselves and rubbing their heads against tree trunks or other stationary objects. Young ride on their mother's back after weaning.

Opossums can defend themselves against large predators and survive substantial injuries. One study showed nearly half of all examined dead opossums had healed broken bones, some with multiple fractures. Many opossums are immune to venomous snake bites and have a resistance to rabies and plague.

Kit Fox
Vulpes macrotis

Family: Wolves, Foxes, and Coyote (Canidae)

Size: L 15–21" (38–53 cm); T 9–12" (23–30 cm); H 10–12" (25–30 cm)

Weight: 3–7 lb. (1.4–3.2 kg)

Description: Yellowish tan fox with a dark line down the back and onto tail. White chin and upper neck. White to tan on the belly. Extremely large, pointed ears. Long thin legs, same color as the body.

Origin/Age: native; 5–10 years

Compare: The Swift Fox (pg. 259) is very similar, but has a shorter tail, shorter muzzle, and slightly smaller ears. Best to use range to help distinguish the Kit from the Swift. The Gray Fox (pg. 263) is larger, darker, and has shorter ears. Red Fox (pg. 267) is larger and has red fur with a white-tipped tail.

Habitat: deserts, semideserts, canyons, grasslands, open fields

Home: underground den, sometimes a hollow log or in a hillside or stream bank, with 3–4 entrances, often with a dirt mound up to 3' (0.9 m) high with scat and scraps of food in front of main entrance; may have several den sites in its territory

Food: omnivore; small mammals such as rabbits, hares, mice, moles, woodrats, and voles; also eats fish, berries, apples, nuts, insects, and carrion

Sounds: hoarse high-pitched barks, yelps to steady high-pitched screams, mournful cries

Breeding: winter (Jan–Mar) mating; 51–53 days gestation

Young: 1–8 kits once per year in April or May

Signs: cylindrical scat with a tapered end, frequently contains hair and bones, often found on a trail, prominent rock or stump, or at the den entrance

Activity: mainly nocturnal, crepuscular; active around the den site at sunrise and sunset, but can also be seen there during the day, sunning itself

Tracks: forepaw 1½" (4 cm) long, oval, with hind paw slightly smaller; 4 toes on each foot, straight line of single tracks; hind paws fall near or directly onto fore prints (direct register) when walking, often obliterating the forepaw tracks, 8–12" (20–30 cm) stride when walking

Stan's Notes: Federally listed as an endangered species. Numbers were reduced in the past by loss of habitat and excessive trapping for its fur. Range extends from California, Nevada, Arizona, and New Mexico to Texas and farther south into Mexico. Was once considered the same species as the Swift Fox (pg. 259).

Considered the smallest of our wild dogs, with the approximate size of a house cat. A highly specialized fox, surviving in both desert and semidesert environments. Does not require a constant supply of fresh water, obtaining all the moisture it needs from its prey and by water conservation, achieved through the production of a specialized urine that is low in water content.

Diet consists of small rodents such as kangaroo rats, but will also take rabbits. Fleet of foot, it runs very fast for short distances, enabling capture of other swift prey such as hares. Travels several miles from the den to hunt for food. Territories overlap only rarely.

Primarily nocturnal, but can be seen during the daylight hours, especially near the den site. Digs its own den (semifossorial) as far down as 8 feet (2.4 m), fashioning it with many entrances. Does not hibernate. Mates pair up in late winter when females clean out dens and get ready to breed. Young first emerge at the den entrance at 5–6 weeks of age. Some report that helper females take part in raising the young of older females.

Some pairs have long-term pair bonds; others don't. Males will bring food to the female while she is nursing young. At weaning, both adults hunt for food and bring it back to the den. Parents carry prey whole to the den and don't regurgitate food.

Swift Fox
Vulpes velox

Family: Wolves, Foxes, and Coyote (Canidae)

Size: L 15–21" (38–53 cm); T 9–12" (23–30 cm); H 10–12" (25–30 cm)

Weight: 3–7 lb. (1.4–3.2 kg)

Description: Yellowish tan fox with a grayish back and sides. White chin and upper neck. White to tan on the belly. Large pointed ears. Small dark marks in front of each eye. Long, bushy black-tipped tail.

Origin/Age: native; 5–10 years

Compare: Kit Fox (pg. 255) has a longer tail, larger muzzle, and taller ears; Kit is less common and seen in western Texas unlike the Swift, which is found in the panhandle. Gray Fox (pg. 263) is larger, darker, and has shorter ears. Red Fox (pg. 267) is larger and has red fur with a white-tipped tail.

Habitat: semideserts, grasslands, prairies, open fields

Home: underground den, in a hillside, cliff, or bank of a stream, 3–4 entrances, often a dirt mound up to 3' (1 m) high at the main entrance with scat and food scraps; may have several dens in its territory

Food: carnivorous; small animals such as rabbits, hares, mice, moles, woodrats, and voles; also eats carrion and insects

Sounds: hoarse high-pitched barks, yelps, high-pitched screams, mournful cries

Breeding: winter (Dec–Feb) mating; 50–53 days gestation

Young: 1–8 kits once per year in March, April, or early May; born helpless with eyes closed

mother and kits

Signs: cylindrical scat with a tapered end, frequently contains hair and bones, often found on a trail, prominent rock or stump, or at the den entrance

Activity: mainly nocturnal, crepuscular; can be seen during the day around the den site, sunning itself

Tracks: forepaw 1½" (4 cm) long, oval, with hind paw slightly smaller; 4 toes on each foot, straight line of single tracks; hind paws fall near or directly onto fore prints (direct register) when walking, often obliterating the forepaw tracks, 8–12" (20–30 cm) stride when walking

Stan's Notes: This is a rare species in Texas. Was almost driven to extinction due to indiscriminate poisoning and shooting. Now protected and the populations seem to be rebounding.

Once considered the same species as the Kit Fox (pg. 255), but now is a separate species. The Swift Fox is by far more common in Texas than the Kit and occurs in the panhandle, where there is flat terrain or gentle rolling hills. Often associated with prairie dog towns and jackrabbits in grasslands.

Unlike the Red Fox (pg. 267) or Gray Fox (pg. 263), the Swift is largely carnivorous, feeding mainly on cottontail rabbits and also jackrabbits, which are nearly the same size as itself, if not slightly taller. When a Swift catches more than it can eat, it will cache the food in shallow depressions, covering the leftovers with scant dirt. Rarely, if ever, takes chickens or other large birds, thus it can make a good neighbor by controlling populations of small rodents, which often eat a lot of grain.

Does not hibernate. Usually seen in pairs and occasionally with more adults together. It is unclear whether or not Swift Foxes mate for life. An excellent digger (semifossorial), it creates several dens and moves its young from den to den when they are old enough to follow their parents.

The young are born helpless with eyes closed. They grow quickly, opening their eyes at 10–14 days and appearing aboveground at 4–5 weeks of age. They learn to hunt from their parents and are dispersed from their home den at the end of their first summer. Young females are capable of breeding in their first year.

Gray Fox

Urocyon cinereoargenteus

Family: Wolves, Foxes, and Coyote (Canidae)

Size: L 22–24" (56–61 cm); T 10–17" (25–43 cm); H 14–15" (36–38 cm)

Weight: 7–13 lb. (3.2–5.9 kg)

Description: Grizzled gray fox with a rust red nape, shoulders, and rust red across the chest. Large pointed ears, trimmed in white. White chin, neck, and belly. Large bushy tail with a black tip and ridge of stiff dark hairs along the top.

Origin/Age: native; 5–10 years

Compare: The Red Fox (pg. 267) has a white-tipped tail. Coyote (pg. 271) shares the grayish appearance and black-tipped tail, but is larger than the Gray Fox and has longer legs.

Habitat: desert scrub, forests, rocky outcrops, river valleys, brushy areas

Home: den, mostly in a natural cavity such as a log or a crevice in rock, will enlarge a prairie dog burrow, unlike a Red Fox den, the den of a Gray Fox lacks a mound of dirt in front of the entrance

Food: omnivore; small mammals such as mice, moles, voles, rabbits, and hares; also eats berries, apples, nuts, fish, insects, and carrion

Sounds: hoarse high-pitched barks, yelps to steady high-pitched screams, mournful cries; much less vocal than the Red Fox

Breeding: winter (Jan–Mar) mating; 51–53 days gestation

Young: 1–7 kits once per year in April or May; born helpless with black fur and eyes closed

Signs: urine and piles of feces, mostly on conspicuous landmarks such as a prominent rock, stump or trail; cylindrical scat with a tapered end, can be very dark if berries were eaten, often contains hair and bones

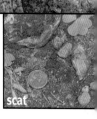
scat

Activity: mostly nocturnal, crepuscular; can be seen during the day in winter, especially when overcast

Tracks: forepaw 1½" (4 cm) long, oval, hind paw slightly smaller; straight line of single tracks; hind paws fall near or directly onto fore prints (direct register) when walking, often obliterating the forepaw tracks, 10–14" (25–36 cm) stride when walking

Stan's Notes: This is by far the most common and widespread fox species in the state. It is more common in eastern Texas than in western parts.

The scientific name provides a very good description of the animal. The genus *Urocyon* is Greek for "tailed dog." The species *cinereoargenteus* is Latin and means "silver" or "gray and black."

Also called Treefox because it often climbs trees. Climbs to escape larger predators more than it does to find food. Sometimes it will rest in a tree. Shinnies up, pivoting its front legs at the shoulder joints to grab the trunk and pushes with hind feet. Able to rotate its front legs more than other canids. Once up the trunk, it jumps from branch to branch and has been seen up to 20 feet (6.1 m) high. Descends by backing down or running headfirst down a sloping branch.

Thought to mate for life. Male often travels 50 miles (81 km) to establish territory. A pair will defend a territory of 2–3 square miles (5–8 sq. km).

The kits are weaned at about six weeks. Male doesn't enter the den, but helps feed the family by bringing in food. Young disperse at the end of summer just before the parents start mating again.

Red Fox
Vulpes vulpes

Family: Wolves, Foxes, and Coyote (Canidae)

Size: L 22–24" (56–61 cm); T 13–17" (33–43 cm); H 15–16" (38–40 cm)

Weight: 7–15 lb. (3.2–6.8 kg)

Description: Usually rusty red with dark highlights, but can vary from light yellow to black. Large pointed ears trimmed in black with white inside. White jowls, chest, and belly. Legs nearly black. Large bushy tail with a white tip. Fluffy coat in winter and spring. Molts by July, appearing smaller and thinner.

Origin/Age: native; 5–10 years

Compare: Gray Fox (pg. 263) is not as red and has a black-tipped tail. Smaller than the Coyote (pg. 271), usually more red and has a white-tipped tail. All other wild canids lack a tail with a white tip.

Habitat: woodlands, scrublands, rangelands, grasslands, prairies, foothills, mountains, suburbs, cities

Home: den, sometimes a hollow log, may dig a den under a log or a rock in a bank of a stream or in a hillside created when land was cut to build a road, often has a mound of dirt up to 3' (0.9 m) high in front of the main entrance with scat deposits

Food: omnivore; small mammals such as mice, moles, voles, rabbits, and hares; also eats berries, apples, nuts, fish, insects, and carrion

Sounds: hoarse high-pitched barks, yelps to steady high-pitched screams, mournful cries

Breeding: winter (Jan–Mar) mating; 51–53 days gestation

Young: 1–10 kits once per year in April or May

summer coat

winter coat

silver morph   dark morph

Signs: cylindrical scat with a tapered end, can be very dark if berries were eaten, frequently contains hair and bones, often found on a trail, prominent rock or stump or at den entrance

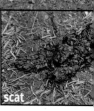

scat

Activity: mainly nocturnal, crepuscular; rests during the middle of the night

Tracks: forepaw 2" (5 cm) long, oval, with hind paw slightly smaller; straight line of single tracks; hind paws fall near or directly onto fore prints (direct register) when walking, often obliterating the forepaw tracks, 10–14" (25–36 cm) stride when walking

Stan's Notes: The most widely distributed wild canid in the world, ranging across North America, Europe, Asia, and northern Africa. Some European Red Foxes were introduced into North America in the 1790s, resulting in confusion regarding the original distribution and lineage. Other individuals are thought to have been introduced into Texas in 1895 for sport hunting and trapping.

den entrance

Usually alone. Very intelligent and learns from past experiences. Often catlike in behavior, pouncing onto prey. Curls up into a ball and sleeps at the base of a tree or rock, even during winter.

Hunts for mice, moles, and other small prey by stalking, looking, and listening. Hearing differs from the other mammals. Hears low-frequency sounds, enabling it to detect small mammals digging and gnawing underground. Chases larger prey such as rabbits and squirrels. Hunts even if full, caching extra food underground. Finds cached food by memory and using its sense of smell.

While mated pairs actively defend their territory from other foxes, they are often killed by coyotes or wolves. Uses a den only several weeks for birthing and raising young. Parents bring food to kits in the den. At first, parents regurgitate the food. Later they bring fresh meat and live prey to the den, where the kits practice killing. Young are dispersed at the end of their first summer, with the males (dog foxes) traveling 100–150 miles (161–242 km)—much farther than females (vixens)—to establish their own territories.

kits

Coyote
Canis latrans

Family: Wolves, Foxes, and Coyote (Canidae)

Size: L 3–3½' (0.9–1.1 m); T 12–15" (30–38 cm); H 18–24" (45–61 cm)

Weight: 20–40 lb. (9–18 kg)

Description: Tan fur with black and orange highlights. Large, pointed reddish orange ears with white interior. Long narrow snout with a white upper lip. Long legs and bushy black-tipped tail.

Origin/Age: native; 5–10 years

Compare: Smaller than Gray Wolf (pg. 279), with larger ears and a narrower pointed snout. The Red Fox (pg. 267) has black legs and a white-tipped tail.

Habitat: urban, suburban and rural areas, scrublands, deserts, mountains, forests, fields, farms

Home: den, usually in a riverbank, hillside, under a rock or tree root, entrance 12–24" (30–61 cm) high, can be up to 30' (9.1 m) deep, and ends in small chamber where female gives birth; female may dig own den or enlarge a fox or badger den

Food: omnivore; small mammals, reptiles, amphibians, birds, bird eggs, insects, fruit, carrion

Sounds: barks like a dog, calls to others result in a chorus of high-pitched howling and yipping; sounds different from the lower, deeper call of the Gray Wolf, which rarely yips

Breeding: mid to late winter; 63 days average gestation

Young: 4–6 pups once per year in April or May; born with eyes closed

summer coat

scat

Signs: cylindrical scat (shape is similar to that of domestic dog excrement), often containing fur and bones, along well-worn game trails, on prominent rocks and at trail intersections

Activity: nocturnal, crepuscular, diurnal; can be seen for several hours after sunrise as well as before sunset

Tracks: forepaw 2¼" (5.5 cm) long, round to slightly oval, hind paw slightly smaller; straight line of single tracks; hind paws fall near or directly onto fore prints (direct register) when walking, often obliterating the forepaw tracks, 12–15" (30–38 cm) stride when walking, 24–30" (61–76 cm) stride when running

Stan's Notes: Sometimes called Brush Wolf or Prairie Wolf, even though this animal is obviously not a wolf. The genus name Canis is Latin for "dog." The species name *latrans* is also Latin and means "barking." It is believed that the common name "Coyote" comes from the Aztec word *coyotl*, which means "barking dog."

Frequently seen as a gluttonous outlaw, this animal is only guilty of being able to survive a rapidly changing environment and outright slaughter by people. Intelligent and playful, much like the domestic dog. Hunts alone or in small groups. Uses its large ears to hear small mammals beneath vegetation. Stands over a spot, cocks its head back and forth to pinpoint prey and then pounces. Will also chase larger prey such as rabbits.

Most coyotes run with their tails down unlike dogs and wolves, which run with their tails level to upright. A fast runner, it can travel 25–30 mph (40–48 km/h). May reach 40 mph (64 km/h) for short distances. Some coyotes tracked with radio collars are known to travel more than 400 miles (644 km) over several days.

Often courts for 2–3 months before mating. A monogamous animal, with mated pairs staying together for many years or for life.

Pups emerge from the den at 2–3 weeks and are weaned at 5–7 weeks. Mother will move her pups from the den when she feels threatened. Mother often gets help raising young from other group members and her mate. Pups do not return to the den once they are able to survive on their own. Mother abandons the den once the pups leave and will often return year after year in spring to use the same den.

Red Wolf
Canis rufus

Family: Wolves, Foxes, and Coyote (Canidae)

Size: L 4–4½' (1.2–1.4 m); T 14–17" (36–43 cm); H 24–36" (61–91 cm)

Weight: 40–80 lb. (18–36 kg)

Description: Usually gray with dark highlights. Reddish tinge, especially on upper legs and face. Large bushy tail, black-tipped. Long pointed ears, widely spaced, with rusty backs. Narrow muzzle and large nose pad. Wide band of white around lips. Long legs and large feet. Male is slightly larger than female.

Origin/Age: native; 5–15 years

Compare: Coyote (pg. 271) is smaller, with shorter legs and a narrow white lip mark. The Red Wolf often holds its tail straight out when traveling; Coyote holds its tail downward. Gray Wolf (pg. 279) has a variety of colors and longer legs.

Habitat: forests, brushlands, grasslands, coastal prairies

Home: shelter or den only for raising young, den can be 5–15' (1.5–4.6 m) deep, frequently more than 1 entrance, fan of dirt at entrance, often scattered bones and fur laying about; used for many years

Food: omnivore; mice, rabbits, hares, deer, and bears; also eats berries, grass, insects, and fish

Sounds: barks and howls, low deep howling may rise and fall in pitch or remain the same; rarely has a series of yips or yelps at the end, like the Coyote

Breeding: Jan–Feb mating; 63–65 days gestation

Young: 2–5 pups once a year; born helpless, eyes closed

Signs: scrapes in the dirt; urine on posts, rocks, and stumps; scat looks like the excrement of a domestic dog, but it is larger and contains hairs and bone fragments

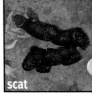
scat

Activity: nocturnal, more diurnal in winter

Tracks: forepaw 5½–6½" (14–16 cm) long, hind paw slightly smaller, both round with clear claw marks; straight line of single tracks; hind paws fall near or directly onto fore prints (direct register) when walking, often obliterating the forepaw tracks, 15–30" (38–76 cm) stride; rarely walks along roads like a domestic dog

Stan's Notes: Once ranged in pockets across the Southeast and eastern Texas. Due to land use changes over the years, persecution by people, and increased coyote populations, Red Wolves in the Lone Star State quickly declined. It is now believed not to be found in Texas (extirpated). To complicate matters, Red Wolves interbreed with coyotes, resulting in a hybrid that more closely resembles a coyote than a wolf, thus repressing the genetic identity of the Red Wolf. To keep a healthy Red Wolf population, coyotes need to be controlled in the area where the Red Wolf exists.

The last pure Red Wolf in Texas was found along the Gulf coast, south of Houston, in extreme southeastern Texas and Louisiana in the 1970s. It is thought that this population is gone. Although many people report seeing this species in Texas, to date none of the reports have been verified. With so many coyotes in Texas it seems most likely the animals sighted are actually coyotes. It is believed the success of the coyote is due to it filling the niche that the Red Wolf once occupied.

The entire wild population of Red Wolf, nearly 100 individuals, is in North Carolina. Reintroduction into North Carolina began in the late 1980s along the Great Smoky Mountains. A small population is kept in captivity for reintroduction purposes.

Like other wolves, this one travels great distances in its territory. Consumes 2–5 pounds (0.9–2.3 kg) of meat per day, but can go for weeks without food. Feeds mainly on small animals such as rabbits, rats, mice, raccoons, and birds.

Packs have a well-defined hierarchy, with one male leader called alpha and his female mate, also alpha. Young are subordinate to adults and make up the rest of the pack. Red Wolves run in smaller packs than Gray Wolves (pg. 279). Unlike the Gray Wolf, young Red Wolves of the previous year do not help to raise the young of the new year.

Gray Wolf
Canis lupus

EXTIRPATED
no longer found

FORMER RANGE

Family: Wolves, Foxes, and Coyote (Canidae)

Size: L 4–5' (1.2–1.5 m); T 14–20" (36–50 cm); H 26–38" (66–96 cm)

Weight: 55–130 lb. (25–59 kg)

Description: Usually gray with dark highlights, but can vary from all white to entirely black. A large bushy tail, almost always black-tipped. Short pointed ears with a wide space between. Long legs and huge feet. Male is slightly larger than female.

Origin/Age: native; 5–15 years

Compare: Larger than the Coyote (pg. 271) and has longer legs, larger feet, and shorter ears. Often holds its tail straight out when traveling unlike Coyote, which holds its tail at a downward angle.

Habitat: forests, brushlands, grasslands, open country

Home: shelter or den only for raising young, den can be 5–15' (1.5–4.6 m) deep, frequently more than 1 entrance, fan of dirt at entrance, often scattered bones and fur laying about; used for many years

Food: omnivore; mammals such as mice, rabbits, hares, deer, and bears; also berries, grass, insects, and fish

Sounds: yelps, barks, and howls; howling may rise and fall in pitch or remain the same; rarely has a series of yips or yelps at the end, like the Coyote

Breeding: Jan–Feb mating; 63–65 days gestation

Young: 1–8 pups once per year; born helpless with eyes closed, wide range of color variations, some look like the parents, others are completely different

white morph

black morph

gray morph

pups

scat

Signs: scrapes in the dirt; urine on posts, rocks, and stumps; scat looks like the excrement of a domestic dog, but it is larger and contains hairs and bone fragments

Activity: nocturnal, more diurnal in winter; hunts at night in summer

Tracks: forepaw 5½–6½" (14–16 cm) long, hind paw slightly smaller, both round with clear claw marks; straight line of single tracks; hind paws fall near or directly onto fore prints (direct register) when walking, often obliterating the forepaw tracks, 15–30" (38–76 cm) stride; rarely walks along roads like a domestic dog

Stan's Notes: The largest wild dog species in North America. Once seen across the nation, it was exterminated from Texas and most other places except for states such as Alaska, Minnesota, Wisconsin, and Michigan. The last authenticated reports of it in Texas were in December 1970. Reintroduced into New Mexico, Arizona, and elsewhere starting in 1998, with the first litter born in the wild from wild parents occurring in 2002. As of 2007 there were only about 50–60 of these wolves in the wild between Arizona and New Mexico. There has been some discussion of reintroducing the Gray Wolf to Big Bend National Park.

One of the most mobile animals, traveling great distances to find food each day. Eats 3–5 pounds (1.4–2.3 kg) of meat per day, but can go weeks without food. May cache large prey items. Not a good long distance runner, but able to achieve speeds of 30 mph (48 km/h) for short distances. A good swimmer, following prey into the water or swimming to islands in lakes and rivers. Communicates by howling, body posturing, and scent marking.

Shies away from people, but this is a social animal, living in packs of 2–15 individuals that consist primarily of family members. The pack has a well-defined hierarchy with a sole male leader called alpha and his female mate, also alpha.

Territory of a pack covers 100–300 square miles (260–780 sq. km). Often uses the same well-worn trails in some areas. Territories of other packs may overlap. Conflicts rarely occur if food is plentiful.

Packs chase down prey or ambush. Dominant members feed first. Some adults bring food back in their stomachs to pups, since the mothers won't leave them the first month. Pups mob feeder adults and lick their faces, encouraging regurgitation. When the pups are older, some wolves baby-sit while the alpha pair goes hunting with the pack. Young join the pack to hunt in the fall of their first year and leave at 2–3 years to form their own pack or join another. After the pups leave, the pack will rendezvous before and after hunting, usually at a grassy area with a good view of the surroundings.

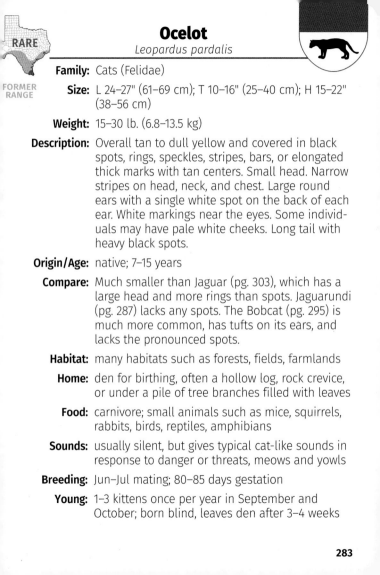

Ocelot
Leopardus pardalis

Family: Cats (Felidae)

Size: L 24–27" (61–69 cm); T 10–16" (25–40 cm); H 15–22" (38–56 cm)

Weight: 15–30 lb. (6.8–13.5 kg)

Description: Overall tan to dull yellow and covered in black spots, rings, speckles, stripes, bars, or elongated thick marks with tan centers. Small head. Narrow stripes on head, neck, and chest. Large round ears with a single white spot on the back of each ear. White markings near the eyes. Some individuals may have pale white cheeks. Long tail with heavy black spots.

Origin/Age: native; 7–15 years

Compare: Much smaller than Jaguar (pg. 303), which has a large head and more rings than spots. Jaguarundi (pg. 287) lacks any spots. The Bobcat (pg. 295) is much more common, has tufts on its ears, and lacks the pronounced spots.

Habitat: many habitats such as forests, fields, farmlands

Home: den for birthing, often a hollow log, rock crevice, or under a pile of tree branches filled with leaves

Food: carnivore; small animals such as mice, squirrels, rabbits, birds, reptiles, amphibians

Sounds: usually silent, but gives typical cat-like sounds in response to danger or threats, meows and yowls

Breeding: Jun–Jul mating; 80–85 days gestation

Young: 1–3 kittens once per year in September and October; born blind, leaves den after 3–4 weeks

Signs: claw scratches on a post up to 3–4' (0.9–1.2 m) tall, scent posts marked with urine; cylindrical scat up to 2–3" (5–7.5 cm) long and ½" (1 cm) wide, contains hair and bones

Activity: nocturnal, diurnal; rests for several hours during the day, especially if it is hot, in a sheltered spot such as under a fallen log, beneath a shrub, or in a rock crevice

Tracks: forepaw and hind paw 2–2½" (5–6 cm), round, heel pad smooth, toes evenly spread, lacking claw marks; straight line of tracks; hind paws fall near or onto fore prints (direct register) when walking, often obliterating the forepaw tracks, 9–10" (23–25 cm) stride

Stan's Notes: A very uncommon cat species in Texas, having estimates of fewer than a couple hundred individuals. Almost all have come up from Mexico looking for new territory and hunting opportunities. Constantly on the move in search of food. Adapts to a wide variety of habitats from rainforest to open desert. Some form of cover is about the only requirement.

Breeding takes place year-round in tropical regions, with females becoming sexually mature at 18 months. Females provide all parental care. It is believed that in Texas breeding takes place in the summer, with 1–2 young, rarely 3, produced during autumn. Polygynous, males mate with all females in or near their territory.

The males have larger territories than the females, 7 square miles (18 sq. km). Females occupy 4⅕ square miles (11 sq. km), but range size varies and depends on the available food supply.

Best known for its pelt, which was the mainstay of the fur trade for many years. At one time more than 200,000 ocelots per year were killed to make coats from their pelts. Today laws prohibit hunting for the fur trade and ocelot coats are a thing of the past.

Primarily nocturnal and solitary, it is occasionally confused with domestic house cats. Mice and other small rodents are the main diet and hunting for them takes place at night. Sometimes it will take a bird, but since most birds are inactive at night this is much less common.

mother and kittens

Jaguarundi
Puma yagouaroundi

RARE

Family: Cats (Felidae)

Size: L 27–33" (69–84 cm); T 12–20" (30–50 cm); H 13–19" (33–48 cm)

Weight: 10–20 lb. (4.5–9 kg)

Description: A uniformly colored cat that occurs in 2 distinct colors, reddish brown or gray, which sometimes appears black. Small, flattened, elongated head, and small pointed ears. Long tail, matching the color of fur on the body. Silver-tipped fur of the dark morph gives it a grizzled appearance.

Origin/Age: native; 7–15 years

Compare: Similar size as Bobcat (pg. 295), which is much more common, has tufts on its ears, and lacks the long tail. Ocelot (pg. 283) is similar in size, but has spots.

Habitat: many habitats such as fields, ranchlands, mesquite, deserts, thorny thickets

Home: den for giving birth, often in a hollow log, rock crevice, or under a pile of tree branches filled with leaves

Food: carnivore; small animals such as mice, squirrels, rabbits, birds, reptiles, amphibians

Sounds: usually silent, but gives typical cat-like sounds in response to danger or threats, meows and yowls

Breeding: any time of year; 65–70 days gestation

Young: 1–3 (usually 2) kittens 1–2 times per year

dark morph

Signs: claw scratches on posts up to 24–36" (30–91 cm) tall, scent posts marked with urine; cylindrical scat up to 1–2" (2.5–5 cm) long and ¼" (0.6 cm) wide, contains hair and bones

Activity: nocturnal, diurnal; rests for several hours during the day, especially if it is hot, in a sheltered spot such as under a fallen log, beneath a shrub, or in a rock crevice

Tracks: forepaw and hind paw 1½–1¾" (4–4.5 cm), round, heel pad smooth, toes evenly spread, lacking claw marks; straight line of tracks; hind paws fall close to or onto the fore prints (direct register) when walking, often obliterating forepaw tracks, 6–9" (15–23 cm) stride

Stan's Notes: A small cat with a unique shape, having a flattened, elongated head and shorter front legs than hind legs, making it look as though it is perpetually going downhill. Not well studied, so solid biological information is in short supply. However, the genus, formerly *Felis*, has been changed to *Puma*.

Very secretive, with a range from South and Central America into southern Arizona and the tip of southern Texas. There are no known breeding populations north of Mexico, but occasionally a single jaguarundi is seen. It is possible that some of these are the offspring of feral house cats. There are also reports of captive jaguarundi escaping and living in the wild.

In Texas the entire population, thought to consist of fewer than 20 individuals, occurs in the lower Rio Grande Valley. Several agencies are working to restore or reintroduce the species into southern Texas. Considered endangered and is fully protected.

Apparently doesn't mind water and occasionally swims to cross rivers. Solitary throughout most of the year, with males seeking females for mating.

One of the few cat species in which offspring of the same litter can be different color morphs. Kittens are born with light spots, which soon fade with age.

Margay
Leopardus wiedii

Family: Cats (Felidae)

Size: L 31–33" (79–84 cm); T 12–20" (30–50 cm); H 15–20" (38–50 cm)

Weight: 7–15 lb. (3.2–6.8 kg)

Description: A small yellow wildcat covered with many dark, irregularly shaped spots, sometimes with lighter colored centers. Small head with short rounded ears, a slender body, and long tail. Belly is lighter with brown spots. Some spots are long and look like stripes, especially around the neck and upper shoulders.

Origin/Age: non-native; 7–12 years

Compare: Similar size as Bobcat (pg. 295), which is much more common, has tufts on its ears, and lacks the long tail. The Ocelot (pg. 283) is smaller and has dark spots with light brown centers and a heavier or stockier body.

Habitat: forests of tropical Central and South America

Home: den for giving birth, in a hollow log, rock crevice, or under a pile of tree branches

Food: carnivore; small animals such as mice, squirrels, rabbits, birds, reptiles, amphibians

Sounds: usually silent, but gives typical cat-like sounds in response to danger or threats, meows and yowls

Breeding: any time of year; 70–84 days gestation

Young: 1–2 kittens 1–2 times per year

Signs: claw scratches on posts up to 3–3¼' (0.9–1 m) tall, scent posts marked with urine; cylindrical scat up to 1–2" (2.5–5 cm) long and ¼" (0.6 cm) wide, contains hair and bones

Activity: nocturnal, diurnal; rests for several hours during the day, especially if it is hot, in a sheltered spot such as under a fallen log, beneath a shrub, or in a rock crevice

Tracks: forepaw and hind paw 2½–3½" (6–9 cm), round, heel pad smooth, toes evenly spread, lacking claw marks; straight line of tracks; hind paws fall close to or onto fore prints (direct register) when walking, often obliterating the forepaw tracks, 7–11" (18–28 cm) stride

Stan's Notes: A small spotted cat of the deep forests of Central and South America. Apparently at one time made its way up into central Mexico. With deforestation it is believed this cat is now very uncommon in Mexico. Considered endangered throughout its range.

The Margay is included in this field guide because of a single specimen taken near Eagle Pass in Maverick County, sometime before 1852. This specimen had an unusual spot pattern and coat. Ancient remains of the species also have been discovered in southern Texas, indicating this cat lived here thousands of years ago during the Pleistocene era.

A skilled climber, scaling trees in search of prey. Known to go down trees headfirst after shinnying up in typical cat fashion.

While the genus was changed from *Felis* to *Leopardus*, not much is known about the Margay. Any suspected sightings should be reported to the Texas Parks and Wildlife Department.

Bobcat
Lynx rufus

Family: Cats (Felidae)

Size: L 2¼–3½' (69–107 cm); T 3–7" (7.5–18 cm); H 18–24" (45–61 cm)

Weight: 14–30 lb. (6.3–13.5 kg)

Description: Tawny brown during summer. Light gray during winter with dark streaks and spots. Long stiff fur projects down from jowls and tapers to a point (cheek ruffs). Triangular ears, tipped with short black hairs (tufts). Prominent white spot on the back of ears. Dark horizontal barring on upper legs. Short stubby tail with a black tip on the top and sides and a white underside. Male slightly larger than female.

Origin/Age: native; 10–15 years

Compare: Much smaller than the Mountain Lion (pg. 299), which has a long rope-like tail. Ocelot (pg. 283) and Jaguarundi (pg. 287) are smaller and not regularly seen in Texas. Look for ear tufts and a white underside of tail to help identify Bobcat.

Habitat: wide variety, mixed forests, fields, farmlands

Home: den, often in a hollow log, rock crevice, or under a pile of tree branches filled with leaves

Food: carnivore; medium to small mammals such as rabbits and mice; also eats birds and carrion

Sounds: raspy meows and yelps, purrs when content

Breeding: Feb–Mar mating; 60–70 days gestation

Young: 1–7 (usually 3) kittens once per year in April or May

Signs: scratching posts with claw marks 3–4' (0.9–1.2 m) aboveground, caches of larger kills covered with a light layer of leaves and twigs, scent posts marked with urine; long cylindrical scat, contains hair and bones, often buried, sometimes visible beneath a thin layer of dirt and debris

scat

Activity: nocturnal, diurnal; often rests on hot days in a sheltered spot such as under a fallen log or in a rock crevice

Tracks: forepaw and hind paw 2" (5 cm), round, multi-lobed heel pad, 4 toes on all feet, lacking claw marks; straight line of tracks; hind paws fall near or on fore prints (direct register) when walking, often obliterating forepaw tracks, 9–13" (23–33 cm) stride

Stan's Notes: This is the most common wildcat species in Texas. Much more common than all the cats found in the state, thriving in nearly all habitat types. The common name refers to the short, stubby or "bobbed" tail. Frequently walks with tail curled upward, which exposes the white underside, making this animal easy to identify. Makes sounds similar to a house cat.

Often uses the same trails in its territory to patrol for rabbits, which is its favorite food, and other prey. Does not climb trees as much as the Mountain Lion (pg. 299), but swims well. Hunts by stalking or laying in wait to attack (ambushing). Ambushes prey by rushing forward, chases and captures it, then kills it with a bite to the neck. Has been known to go without eating for several weeks during periods of famine.

Male has a larger territory than female. Usually solitary except for mating and when mothers are with young. Male will seek out a female in heat. Several males may follow a female until she is ready for mating.

Female does not breed until her second year. She has a primary (natal) den in which kittens are born and live for a short time after birth. Female also has secondary dens in her territory, where she may move her young if the natal den is disturbed. Dens are used only by the females and young. Mother raises young on her own.

kittens

Kittens are born well furred and with spots. Their eyes are closed at birth and open at about 10 days. They are weaned at approximately 8 weeks, when they start to hunt with their mother. Young stay with their mother until about 7 months, when she disperses them to mate.

Mountain Lion
Puma concolor

Family:	Cats (Felidae)
Size:	L 5–6' (1.5–1.8 m); T 24–36" (61–91 cm); H 30–36" (76–91 cm)
Weight:	M 80–267 lb. (36–120 kg); F 64–142 lb. (29–64 kg)
Description:	Overall light to tawny brown with light gray-to-white underside. White upper lip and chin, pink nose, dark spot at base of white whiskers. Small oval ears. Long legs. Large round feet. Long rope-like tail with a dark tip.
Origin/Age:	native; 10–20 years
Compare:	Bobcat (pg. 295) is much smaller, with a short tail. The Jaguar (pg. 303) is slightly larger and covered with spots. Look for a long rope-like tail to help identify the Mountain Lion.
Habitat:	river valleys, woodlands, unpopulated locations
Home:	den, often a sheltered rock crevice, thicket, cave, or other protected place; female uses den only to give birth, male does not use den
Food:	carnivore; larger mammals such as hares, rabbits, opossums, raccoons, javelinas, skunks, and deer
Sounds:	purrs when content or with cubs; growls, snarls, and hisses when threatened or in defense; loud frightening scream during mating; rarely roars
Breeding:	year-round mating; 90–100 days gestation
Young:	1–6 (usually 3) cubs every 2 years; born helpless and blind, covered with dark spots until 3 months, leaves den at 40–70 days and does not return, remains with mother until 15 months

stalking

scat

cubs

Signs: long scratches and gashes above 5' (1.5 m) on larger tree trunks, small piles of urine-soaked dirt and debris (serving as scent posts), caches of uneaten prey covered with small branches and leaves; large cylindrical scat up to 10" (25 cm) long and 2" (5 cm) wide, contains hair and bones, sometimes lightly covered with dirt

Activity: primarily nocturnal, to a lesser extent crepuscular; active all year, usually rests in a tree in daytime, rests near a recent kill

Tracks: forepaw and hind paw 5–6" (13–15 cm), round, lobed heel pad, toes evenly spread, lacks claw marks; straight line of tracks; hind paws fall near or onto fore prints (direct register) when walking, often obliterating forepaw tracks, 12–28" (30–71 cm) stride

Stan's Notes: The Mountain Lion was the most widely ranging cat in the New World in the early 1800s, from Canada to the tip of South America. It was hunted by government professionals to protect livestock from attack until the 1960s. Now only rarely seen in Texas, usually in remote unpopulated areas. Often secretive and avoids humans, but has been known to attack people.

Contrary to the popular belief that it harms the deer population, it usually hunts and kills only about once each week, feeding for many days on the same kill. It hunts by stalking and springing from cover or dropping from a tree. Frequently drags its kill to a secluded area to eat, buries the carcass, and returns to feed over the next couple days, often at night. It is an excellent climber and can leap distances up to 20 feet (6.1 m). Will swim if necessary.

Some people mistakenly think this cat will make a good pet and do not know what to do when their "pet" starts to knock down family members and bite them. These "pets" are released and then often turn up in suburban areas. Usually these are the animals that attack people since they have lost their fear of humans.

Home range of the male is 54–115 square miles (140–299 sq. km) and excludes other male mountain lions. Female range is nearly half the size of the male territory.

Solitary animal except for females with cubs and when mating. During that time the male travels and sleeps with the female for up to a couple weeks. The female matures sexually at 2–3 years of age. Only the females raise the young.

Jaguar
Panthera onca

Family: Cats (Felidae)

Size: L 5–6¼' (1.5–1.9 m); T 17–27" (43–69 cm); H 28–34" (71–86 cm)

Weight: 75–325 lb. (34–146 kg)

Description: Overall tan to yellow and covered in black spots or rings in horizontal rows. Rings have 1–2 small spots inside. A large head with short round ears. Short stout legs. Long, thick rope-like tail with black spots and rings. Legs, head, and tail have solid spots. Rarely entirely black with faint spots. Male slightly larger than female.

Origin/Age: native; 10–20 years

Compare: Mountain Lion (pg. 299) adult is slightly smaller and lacks spots; young lions just have faint spotting. Much larger than Ocelot (pg. 283), which appears more like a house cat and isn't regularly found in Texas.

Habitat: mixed forests, fields, farmlands

Home: den for giving birth, often in a hollow log, rock crevice, or beneath a pile of tree branches filled with leaves

Food: carnivore; medium to large mammals such as rabbits, deer, coatis, javelinas

Sounds: roars, snarls

Breeding: Dec–Jan mating; 93–110 days gestation

Young: 2–4 kittens once per year in April or May; born blind, leaves the den after 3 weeks, can remain with the mother for up to 2 years

Signs: caches of larger kills covered with a light layer of leaves and twigs, scent posts marked with urine; large cylindrical scat up to 10" (25 cm) long and 2" (5 cm) wide, contains hair and bones, sometimes lightly covered with dirt

Activity: nocturnal; rests during the day in a sheltered spot such as under a fallen log or in a rock crevice

Tracks: forepaw 4–4½" (10–11 cm), hind paw 5–6½" (13–16 cm), round, lobed heel pad, toes evenly spread, lacks claw marks; straight line of tracks; hind paws fall near or on the fore prints (direct register) when walking, often obliterating the forepaw tracks, 12–28" (30–71 cm) stride

Stan's Notes: This is the largest and most powerful cat in North, Central, and South America. Third largest cat in the world behind the African lion and tiger. Very rare in Texas. Ranges to Patagonia, South America, and wanders over a very large area, with some jaguars covering 200 square miles (520 sq. km). Always on the move in search of food. Hunts mainly on the ground by stalking and pouncing mostly on large prey such as deer and javelinas.

Where its common name comes from is unclear. South American Natives reportedly call it a fierce dog or large-bodied dog. Its jaws are more powerful than those of the Mountain Lion (pg. 299), enabling it to feed on very large animals and even to bite through their skulls.

A good climber, but does not spend as much time in trees as the Mountain Lion. Unlike other cats, it loves water and is a good swimmer, often resting while half submerged. Solitary except for the breeding season, when males seek females. With such large territories and so few individuals, many do not breed every year. Reports of males staying with females and even bringing food to the young for the first year are not substantiated.

Young stay with their mother and start to hunt at age 6 months; some individuals stay with the mother for up to 24 months. The young are dispersed by the mother when she is ready to breed again. Young become sexually mature at 3 years of age.

Revered by many Indigenous peoples. The Mayans believed it to be the god of the underworld, helping the sun to travel underneath the earth at night, ensuring it would rise each morning.

All-black jaguars (melanistic) occur, but they are uncommon and may be found only in dark jungle habitats in the wild. In some individuals spots are sometimes still visible. These individuals are known as Black Panthers, but they are not a separate species. Any of these animals seen in Texas are probably the result of escape.

Javelina
Pecari tajacu

Family: Peccaries (Tayassuidae)

Size: L 3–4' (0.9–1.2); T 1–2" (2.5–5 cm); H 20–24" (50–61 cm)

Weight: 30–60 lb. (13.5–27 kg)

Description: Large thick body and short dark legs. Dark brown to nearly black with a grizzled appearance. Faint, narrow white collar from shoulder to shoulder. Flexible cartilaginous snout like that of domestic pigs. Tiny dark eyes. Small well-furred ears. Very small straight tail, hard to see, not curled like domestic pigs. Straight tusks, 1–2" (2.5–5 cm) long, showing just the tips at the sides of mouth.

Origin/Age: native; 15–20 years

Compare: Domesticated pigs have a coiled tail and do not have dark fur. Feral Pig (pg. 367) is larger, with a less uniform color and tusks pointing upward.

Habitat: open forests, shrublands, semideserts

Home: no den or nest; constantly on the move but never too far from water, rests in the open or under a tree, seeking shelter from the heat

Food: herbivore; prickly pear cacti, mesquite fruit, stool and agave plants, roots, and tubers

Sounds: snorts and grunts, squeals, barking alarm call

Breeding: any time of year; 21 weeks gestation

Young: 1–3 reds once per year; remains red with a dark stripe down the back for up to 3 months, nurses for 3 months, nursing from behind the mother's hind legs while she stands

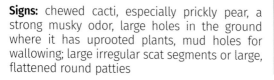

red

tusks

young fighting

Signs: chewed cacti, especially prickly pear, a strong musky odor, large holes in the ground where it has uprooted plants, mud holes for wallowing; large irregular scat segments or large, flattened round patties

scat

Activity: all times; feeds every several hours in winter, resting in between; takes a longer break during the heat of the day in summer, sleeping in the shade of a shrub or tree

Tracks: front hoof ¾–1½" (2–4 cm) long, cloven, pointed in the front, hind hoof slightly smaller; offset line of paired tracks; hind hooves fall near fore prints (no direct register) when walking

Stan's Notes: The javelina (pronounced "HA-veh-LEE-nah") is the only native pig-like animal found in North America. Also known as Collared Peccary, it occurs throughout the American tropics up through Mexico and into southern Texas, Arizona, and parts of New Mexico. While it is the only native wild hooved animal that can breed year-round, numbers are declining in many parts of the Lone Star State.

Wild and domestic pigs came from Europe (Old World) and are only distantly related to javelinas. The javelina has a scent gland on its back above the tail that gives the animal a characteristic smell; pigs do not have this. Javelina tusks are short and straight, pointing down, while pig tusks are curved and point upward. Javelina tails are short, furred, and straight; hog tails are long, naked, and curly. The javelina usually has only 2 offspring at a time, but a pig has up to 20 at one time. Unlike pigs, javelinas are highly social, forming permanent herds with cooperation among the members.

Herds consist of as many as 50 individuals, but smaller groups are more common. All snuggle side by side to help keep warm on cold nights. A dominant male leads the pack and performs all the mating. Young (reds) are protected by the entire herd. Parents break up fights between youngsters.

Has very poor vision, but an excellent sense of smell. Also called Musk Hog due to the scent gland. Each herd has its own unique smell that helps individuals identify other members of the herd. New members are born into the pack and remain for their entire lives. Strangers are rarely taken in.

When a javelina is alarmed, the dark mane stands erect. Always on the move in search of food. Never far from water because it needs to drink often. Usually shy and secretive, but can be tame in suburban areas.

male

Blackbuck

Antilope cervicapra

Family: Goats, Sheep, and Cattle (Bovidae)

Size: L 3½–4' (1.1–1.2 m); T 3–6" (7.5–15 cm); H 30–36" (76–91 cm)

Weight: M 50–90 lb. (23–41 kg); F 40–75 lb. (18–34 kg)

Description: Head, neck, back, and outer legs are dark brown to nearly black. White around eyes and muzzle, lower chest, sides, belly, and inside of legs. Ears are gray to white. Horns are brown, 12–18" (30–45 cm) long, twisted like a corkscrew, and form a V. Female is light brown to tan, has the same color pattern as the male and lacks horns.

Origin/Age: non-native; 10–15 years

Compare: The White-tailed Deer (pg. 355) and Mule Deer (pg. 359) are much larger and lack the twisted straight horns. The Nilgai (pg. 315) is much larger and has a larger, stockier body and shorter horns. The Pronghorn (pg. 331) is larger and has thicker horns that are black.

Habitat: scrublands, grasslands, brushlands, ranches, semideserts

Home: no den or nest; rests in open terrain, does not seek shelter to give birth or escape bad weather

Food: herbivore; grasses and other green plants, brush

Sounds: usually quiet; male snorts and makes other aggressive sounds when competing for females

Breeding: year-round mating; 5–6 months gestation

Young: 1 fawn once per year at any time, but more common in spring and summer; can walk within minutes of birth

female

female

sparring

non-breeding male

Signs: oval depressions in dirt are evidence of beds; scat in groups of small oval pellets

Activity: diurnal, crepuscular; often seen grazing in large open fields, grasslands, and scrublands in early morning or late in the day, almost always in groups

Tracks: front hoof 2" (5 cm) long, hind hoof slightly smaller, both with a split heart shape with the point in the front; neat line of single tracks; hind hooves fall near or directly onto fore prints (direct register) when walking, often obliterating the front hoof tracks, heart shape widens when walking in mud or running

Stan's Notes: A small attractive antelope originally from India, Pakistan, and Nepal that has been introduced into several parts of the world including North and South America. Once abundant and common in its home range, current populations are small and isolated. Despite the fact that it was the most hunted species in India, it is not considered an endangered species there. Still, Blackbuck hunting is strictly prohibited in that country.

In Texas it occurs mainly on Edwards Plateau, where grasslands and brush provide food and shelter. Most Blackbucks in Texas are maintained for hunting on private ranches with high fences.

Almost always found in herds of a dominant male, a harem of females, and young. On average, Blackbucks in the United States are larger than those of the native lands. Blackbucks are thriving so well in this country that some specimens were shipped from Texas to India to help repopulate areas where it was eliminated.

Horns of the male are ringed with 3–4 turns. The horns originate close together at the skull and splay widely, forming a distinct V shape when viewed from the front.

Males take upwards of a couple years to become sexually mature. Females mature in less than a year. Mature males can be very territorial, defending 3–30 acres (1.2–12 ha). Fights and sparring between males can last a long time and cover a large area.

Young males form their own herd and travel together. Once they are sexually mature they move off to establish their own territory and start to collect a harem. Breeding takes place at any time of year, although most occurs in spring and fall. Young are born any time of year, with single fawns being the rule.

male

Nilgai
Boselaphus tragocamelus

Family: Goats, Sheep, and Cattle (Bovidae)

Size: L 5–6½' (1.5–2 m); T 12–15" (30–38 cm); H 4–5'
(1.2–1.5 m)

Weight: M 250–650 lb. (113–293 kg); F 225–475 lb.
(101–214 kg)

Description: Large body and long slender legs. Tan or brown,
turning blue gray to black. Small head and long
snout. Short, slightly curved, pointed horns. Black
chest, belly, and legs. White rings on legs near
hooves. White bib on throat. Narrow beard from
the center of chest, up to 8" (20 cm) long. Female
is light brown with white and black rings around
legs above hooves, and lacks horns.

Origin/Age: non-native; 10–15 years

Compare: Barbary Sheep (pg. 319) has curved horns with
long hair on throat, chest, and upper legs. White-
tailed Deer (pg. 355) and Mule Deer (pg. 359) have
branching antlers. Pronghorn (pg. 331) is much
smaller, with thicker horns that are black.

Habitat: dry scrublands, grasslands, brushlands, ranches

Home: no den; rests in open terrain, does not seek
shelter to give birth or escape bad weather

Food: herbivore; grasses and other green plants, brush

Sounds: usually quiet, but gives a roaring vocalization
when alarmed

Breeding: Dec–Mar mating, but can breed any time of year;
7–8 months gestation

Young: 2 offspring once per year at any time, but more
common in summer; walks minutes after birth

315

female

scat

Signs: oval depressions in dirt are evidence of beds; large scat in frequently visited areas

Activity: diurnal, crepuscular; grazing in large open areas such as grasslands and scrublands, avoiding forested areas, always in groups of 10 or more

Tracks: front and hind hooves 4–5" (10–13 cm) long, split heart shape with the point in the front; neat line of single tracks spaced far apart; hind hooves fall near or directly onto fore prints (direct register) when walking, often obliterating the front hoof tracks, heart shape widens when walking in mud or running

Stan's Notes: This is the largest species of Asian antelope, but not related to our Pronghorn (pg. 331), which is often mistakenly called an antelope. Native to India and Pakistan, the Nilgai was brought to Texas as a game species for private ranches with tall fences. It has since escaped and is now established in the wild, doing well and reproducing on its own. It is the most abundant free-ranging exotic animal in Texas, with populations estimated at 15,000 or more in south central and southern Texas.

The common name "Nilgai" comes from the Hindu word *nilgaw*, which means "blue bull," referring to the color of the mature male. Can be in herds of 5–15, but larger herds have been reported. Also seen traveling alone. Males remain in groups for most of the year, interacting with females only to mate, usually December through March, but breeding can occur any time during the year.

While the Nilgai has good eyesight and excellent hearing similar to that of White-tailed Deer (pg. 355), it does not have a good sense of smell. It is fairly fast, reaching speeds of up to 30 mph (48 km/h) for short distances, and can jump fences.

Coyotes can take young, but adults are predator-free. Apparently this non-native coexists very well with other large mammals in Texas and does not appear to compete or harm native species. However, having only a thin coat of fur and being susceptible to cold temperatures, the Nilgai population is limited mainly by frigid weather.

male

Barbary Sheep
Ammotragus lervia

Family: Goats, Sheep, and Cattle (Bovidae)

Size: L 4–5' (1.2–1.8 m); T 3–6" (7.5–15 cm); H 30–36" (76–91 cm)

Weight: M 225–325 lb. (101–146 kg); F 100–140 lb. (45–63 kg)

Description: Stocky and muscular mammal with a thick neck. Overall light tan to brown. Long brown tail with a tassel at the end. Extremely large horns, slightly curved, ridged, arching backward, sometimes curling down. Long-haired beard extending to the center of chest or upper legs. Short pointed ears. Large brown eyes. May have white around the tip of muzzle. Female is similar in color, but lacks a beard and has shorter back-curving horns.

Origin/Age: non-native; 10–15 years

Compare: Bighorn Sheep (pg. 323) lack the long-haired beard and males have horns that curl back into a full circle. Pronghorn (pg. 331) is found in a different habitat (open range) and males have tall straight horns.

Habitat: dry rough mountains, rocky cliffs

Home: no den or nest; rests on a cliff or ledge, does not seek shelter to give birth or escape bad weather

Food: herbivore; grasses and other green plants in summer, shrubs and other woody plants in winter

Sounds: usually quiet

Breeding: Sep–Nov mating; 5–6 months gestation

Young: 1 lamb once per year in February to April; can walk within minutes of birth

female

Signs: oval depressions in dirt on ledges or cliffs are evidence of beds; scat in many single round pellets when it has consumed dried woody plants, masses of large segmented scat when it has fed on green plants

Activity: crepuscular; feeds for up to several hours in the early part of the day and again late in the day near sunset

Tracks: front hoof 2–2½" (5–6 cm) long, hind hoof slightly smaller, widely split at the front with a point in the front; hind hooves fall near or directly onto fore prints (direct register) when walking, often obliterating the front hoof tracks, widens when walking in mud or running; tracks rarely seen because of the rocky habitat

Stan's Notes: A large exotic-looking sheep that is originally from the mountains of North Africa (Barbary Coast). Also known as Aoudads, its common name in North Africa. The genus name breaks down to *ammos* from the Greek and means "sand," referring to its sand-colored coat, and *tragos* for "goat." Species name *lervia* is from the name of all wild sheep of northern Africa.

Introduced to many parts of Europe and to the United States, in Texas it occurs in the Trans-Pecos region and Palo Duro Canyon, along the Edwards Plateau, on the South Texas Plains and also on private ranches. First released into the wild in the mid–1950s, it is now well established in many areas.

Similar to the Bighorn Sheep (pg. 323), it is an excellent climber, scaling up cliff sides and descending steep slopes with great ease. Since it feeds on similar plants in a similar habitat as the native Bighorn Sheep, it is feared that this non-native species may out-compete the Bighorn if the Barbary population grows too large.

The horns are triangular in cross section and become full size in males within 6–7 years. Can go a long time without freestanding water, obtaining its water needs from the green plants it eats. If freestanding water is available, it will drink freely and also has been known to wallow in it.

Found alone or in small groups comprised of young and old of both sexes. Young females become sexually mature in 1 year, but usually don't breed until they are 2 years of age. The males take longer to mature and only the dominant males breed.

male

Bighorn Sheep
Ovis canadensis

Family: Goats, Sheep, and Cattle (Bovidae)

Size: L 4–6' (1.2–1.8 m); T 3–6" (7.5–15 cm); H 2½–3½' (76–107 cm)

Weight: M 150–320 lb. (68–144 kg); F 100–200 lb. (45- 90 kg)

Description: Muscular with a thick neck. Light tan to brown. White rump. Short dark tail. White-tipped muzzle. Very large horns, curled, heavily ridged, pointing forward. Female is tan to brown with a thin neck, short legs, short oval ears, and short, back-curving horns. Coloring of both sexes varies seasonally.

Origin/Age: native; 10–15 years

Compare: Barbary Sheep (pg. 319) has tufts of long hair on its chest and front legs. Pronghorn (pg. 331) is smaller and males have tall straight horns. Look for the large curled horns of the male or short tan horns of the female to help identify the Bighorn.

Habitat: mountains, rocky cliffs, forests, valleys

Home: no den or nest; rests on a cliff or ledge, does not seek shelter for birthing or bad weather, day beds are 3–4 scratches in the ground, often with fecal pellets and urine, night beds are deeper scrapes

Food: herbivore; grasses and other green plants in summer, shrubs and other woody plants in winter

Sounds: usually quiet

Breeding: Nov–Dec mating; 6 months gestation

Young: 1 lamb once per year in May or June; can walk within minutes of birth, nurses for several weeks, eats forage at 2 weeks, weaned at 5–6 months

ewes and lambs

female

Signs: oval depressions in grass are evidence of beds; scat in single round pellets when it has consumed dried woody plants, masses of large segmented scat when it has fed on green plants

scat

Activity: diurnal; feeds for up to several hours, sits down to rest for up to 2 hours, then feeds again

Tracks: front hoof 2½–3" (6–7.5 cm) long, hind hoof slightly smaller, widely split at the front with a point; neat line of single tracks; hind hooves fall near or directly onto fore prints (direct register) when walking, often obliterating the front hoof tracks, widens when walking in mud or running

Stan's Notes: All Bighorn Sheep in Texas today are the result of reintroduced populations. Formerly ranged in isolated pockets in the Trans-Pecos region. The last native population (now extinct) was seen in the late 1950s. Reintroductions have taken place in the Sierra Diablo-Baylor-Beach Mountains, Van Horn Mountains, Elephant Mountains Wildlife Management Area, and Black Gap Wildlife Management Area. Several subspecies were introduced to Texas; some were originally found in the state (*O. c. mexicana*). While thought of as an animal of high mountains and steep canyons, evidence shows this may be a result of hunting pressures. Historically, it ranged into the foothills and plains.

Also called Mountain Sheep or Bighorns. Massive, heavily ridged horns can be useful in determining the age of an adult male (ram). Horns sweeping back and outward, then forward and curving upward eventually form what is called a full curl. Horn tips are often torn or broken, a condition known as brooming. Rams with full curl horns are 7–8 years of age. Horns of younger rams are shorter and more slender.

A gregarious and social animal, with females (ewes) and young (lambs) forming large herds that travel, feed and play together. Older rams form small bachelor herds.

Rams don't breed until 7–8 years of age, when they have full curl horns, with horn size determining the breeding status. The most dominant ram will do most of the breeding of the ewe herd. Ewes breed at 2–3 years of age.

Rams are well known for butting their heads during the rut. They will charge each other at speeds up to 20 mph (32 km/h), crashing their bony foreheads together, resulting in a very loud crack that can be heard from more than a mile away.

Hooves have a hard bony edge and soft spongy center, allowing the animal to scamper over rocky surfaces with ease. Makes short, seasonal migrations from summer to winter ranges.

male

American Bison
Bison bison

Family: Goats, Sheep, and Cattle (Bovidae)

Size: L 8–12' (2.4–3.7 m); T 12–19" (30–48 cm); H 5–6' (1.5–1.8 m)

Weight: M 1,000–2,000 lb. (450–900 kg); F 800–1,000 lb. (360–450 kg)

Description: Dark brown head, lighter brown body and large humped shoulders. Bearded with a long shaggy mane over head and shoulders. Long tuft-tipped tail. Both sexes have short curved horns, which are not shed.

Origin/Age: native; 20–25 years

Compare: A massive animal, difficult to confuse with any other. No longer roams freely in Texas. Seen only in established, managed areas such as state parks and private ranches.

Habitat: scrublands, semideserts, open forests, mountains

Home: does not use a den or nest, even in bad weather or winter; beds in a different spot each night, rests in the open, laying on the ground

Food: herbivore; grasses and other green plants, lichens

Sounds: often quiet; male bellows during the rut, female snorts, young bawls for mother's attention

Breeding: Jul–Aug mating; 9–10 months gestation

Young: 1 calf every 1–2 years in May or June; born with reddish brown fur, stands within 30 minutes, walks within hours of its birth, joins herd at 2–3 days, acquires hump, horns and adult coloration at 2–3 months, weaned at 6–7 months

flehmening

female

scat

Signs: saucer-like depressions in dirt (wallows), 8–10' (2.4–3 m) wide, trees and shrubs with the bark rubbed off, shallow depressions in the grass are evidence of bison beds; scat is similar to that of the domestic cow, flat round patties, 12–14" (30–36 cm) wide

Activity: crepuscular; often rests during the day to chew its cud

Tracks: front hoof 6–7" (15–18 cm) long, hind hoof slightly smaller, both with opposing crescents and more pointed in the front; hind hooves fall behind and slightly to the side of fore prints; crescents widen when walking in mud or running

Stan's Notes: The largest land mammal in North America and considered unique to the New World. Sometimes called Buffalo, but not related to the Old World buffalo.

Historically, the American Bison ranged throughout most of the United States and numbered in the tens of millions. It was hunted to near extinction around the 1880s, when a government policy advocated extermination. By the early 1900s fewer than 1,000 bison remained in the country.

Bison were once widespread in the western two-thirds of Texas, with extirpation occurring in the late 1800s. Now all bison in the Lone Star State are a result of private herds managed on ranches and state parks.

Centuries ago, great herds of bison would migrate long distances between summer and winter grounds. Because bison are now kept behind fences in managed herds, they no longer migrate.

Gregarious, gathering in large herds of nearly 100 bison, mainly females (cows) and calves. Can be seen rolling and rubbing in wallows to relieve insect bites. Males (bulls) are usually on their own or in a small group in fall and winter. A dominant bull will join a maternal herd late in summer before the rut. Cows mature at 2–3 years and stay fertile for about 24 hours. A bull will curl its upper lip and extend its neck (flehmening) when around cows, perhaps to detect estrus. Bulls "tend" cows that are entering estrus rather than maintaining harems. Competing bulls strut near each other, showing off their large profile. Mature bulls sometimes face each other, charge, crash headfirst and use their massive necks to push each other. Fights rarely result in injury. Sometimes hooking or goring occurs.

sparring

male

Pronghorn

Antilocapra americana

Family: Pronghorn (Antilocapridae)

Size: L 4–4½' (1.2–1.4 m); T 3–7" (7.5–18 cm); H 3–3½' (0.9–1.1 m)

Weight: M 100–140 lb. (45–63 kg); F 75–100 lb. (34–45 kg)

Description: Neck, back, and outer legs are light tan to reddish tan. White patches on chin, neck, chest, sides, and rump. Ears are trimmed in black. Male horns are 12–20" (30–50 cm) long, black, each with a single point curving inward and small tine about halfway up. Female horns are 3–4" (7.5–10 cm) long, black, each with 1 point and lacking a tine.

Origin/Age: native; 5–10 years

Compare: The White-tailed Deer (pg. 355) and Mule Deer (pg. 359) lack white sides and black horns. The Nilgai (pg. 315) has a larger, stockier, dark gray body and single, slightly curved horns. Blackbuck (pg. 311) has very long, twisted horns.

Habitat: scrublands, grasslands, farms, ranches, semideserts

Home: no den or nest; rests in open terrain, does not seek shelter to give birth or escape bad weather

Food: herbivore; grasses and other green plants

Sounds: usually quiet, snorts loudly to show aggression toward another Pronghorn

Breeding: Aug–Oct mating; 7–8 months gestation; implantation delayed until 1 month after mating

Young: 2 offspring once per year in May or June; 3–13 lb. (1.4–5.9 kg), can walk within minutes of birth, grayer than adult, acquires adult coloration at about 1 month

female

scat

Signs: oval depressions in leaves are evidence of beds; scat in groups of small oval pellets when it has eaten woody material, masses of large segmented scat when it has fed on green plants

Activity: diurnal, nocturnal; often seen grazing in large open fields, grasslands and scrublands

Tracks: front hoof 3" (7.5 cm) long, hind hoof slightly smaller, both with a split heart shape with the point in the front; neat line of single tracks; hind hooves fall near or directly onto fore prints (direct register) when walking, often obliterating the front hoof tracks, heart shape widens when walking in mud or running

Stan's Notes: Occurring only in North America (endemic), the Pronghorn is the sole member of its family. It's the only surviving member of a group of a dozen or so species that occurred during the Pleistocene era.

The fastest land animal in North America. Achieves speeds up to 70 mph (113 km/h) for short distances, with a cruising speed of 30–40 mph (48–64 km/h). Will outrun a predator such as a wolf. Can leap about 20 feet (6.1 m) horizontally while running, but reluctant to jump a standard-height barbed wire fence, choosing to crawl underneath it or pass through between the strands.

Also known as the American Antelope, even though it is not an antelope. The common name "Pronghorn" comes from the small tine or prong located halfway up the horns of the male (buck). It has true horns, which are made of hair-like (keratin) sheaths over bony cores, as opposed to antlers. The only horned animal that sheds horns. Horns are shed annually, usually in November or December after the rut. Shed horns break down quickly in the environment and are rarely found. About one-third of females (does) lack horns; the rest have small horns.

Eyesight is said to be eight times better than human sight. Able to spot predators approaching from long distances. Well suited to life on the open range, with herds traveling great distances to find good grazing areas. Can tolerate extremely cold weather.

The buck will gather a harem and start to defend territory during March. If trapped, a buck will fall back behind the herd and fight off the predator with its horns and by kicking.

The doe becomes sexually mature at 16 months. A doe usually produces only one offspring per year for the first couple of years, while an older female will often have twins or sometimes triplets.

Babies spend their first week or so hiding in tall grass, with their mother returning regularly to nurse. The young can outrun most predators at about 1 week of age.

Burro
Equus asinus

Family: Horses (Equidae)

Size: L 4–5' (1.2–1.5 m); T 12–24" (30–61 cm); H 4–4½' (1.2–1.4 m)

Weight: 400–650 lb. (180–293 kg)

Description: Wide variety of colors and patterns, but all have the same general size and shape of a small horse with large ears. May have faint zebra-like striping on the sides. Long snout, often white. Short erect mane, black-tipped tail and stout legs. Dark stripe from mane to tail and across shoulders.

Origin/Age: non-native; 20–35 years

Compare: Smaller than horses. Look for the large ears, large head, short erect mane, and slow calm nature. No branding or other marks. Found in the deserts alone or in small groups in remote wild areas and on public lands.

Habitat: semideserts, deserts, shrublands, valleys

Home: no den or nest; rests in open terrain, does not seek shelter to give birth or escape bad weather

Food: herbivore; grasses and other green plants, small thin twigs

Sounds: typical donkey heehaws, squeals, and snorts

Breeding: any time of year; 12 months (360–370 days) gestation; female becomes sexually mature at 2 years

Young: 1 foal once per year; weighs 20–30 pounds (9–13.5 kg) at birth, able to walk within 30 minutes, nurses for 4–5 months

Signs: oval depressions in grass are evidence of beds; scat in piles of large patties, large amounts of urine, sometimes pooling on flat open ground

Activity: diurnal; feeds for up to several hours before resting for up to 2 hours and feeding again, may take a break at midday

Tracks: front and hind hooves 2–3" (5–7.5 cm) wide, each a large single semicircle; wide space between each print; hind hooves do not register in fore prints

Stan's Notes: A non-native species originally from northern Africa and the Arabian peninsula that was introduced around the world. Rare in Texas. Occurs in deserts and semideserts in small groups consisting of one male, two females, and their young. Herds often break up and reform. Dominant males, usually 3–5 years of age, sometimes defend territories and often tolerate subordinate males.

Also called Donkey, Wild Donkey, or Wild Ass. Closely related to horses and interbreeds with them, producing hybrids. Burros breeding with horses and zebras produce hybrids that cannot reproduce (sterile). A cross between a male burro (jack) and a female horse produces a mule. A cross between a female burro (jenny) and a male horse produces a hinny. A cross between a burro and a zebra produces a zebra or what is known as a zonkey.

Very important to civilizations around the world, playing a role in human economies from the time of the ancient Egyptians to the present. Has been domesticated as a pack animal for about 6,000 years. Capable of carrying more than 200 pounds (30 kg) for extended periods of time. Known to go without food and water for several days.

Most active in early morning and late in the afternoon, when it feeds on grasses. Often rests during midday. Will sleep standing up or laying down. Has excellent vision, keen hearing, and a good sense of smell.

Burros are very observant and cautious animals that will refuse to do anything out of the ordinary or dangerous. This behavior has given them the reputation of being stubborn as a mule. However, most burros that have been domesticated are quite passive and make wonderful companions for both people and horses.

Feral Horse
Equus caballus

Family: Horses (Equidae)

Size: L 5–7' (1.5–2.1 m); T 12–24" (30–61 cm); H 4½–5½' (1.4–1.7 m)

Weight: M 800–900 lb. (360–405 kg); F 550–750 lb. (248–338 kg)

Description: Nearly identical to domestic horses in size, shape, and color, with many colors and patterns. Large powerful body. Long snout. Long mane and tail. May have faint zebra-like striping on the sides.

Origin/Age: non-native; 20–35 years

Compare: Slightly smaller than domestic horses, otherwise extremely hard to differentiate from afar except for its behavior. The Feral Horse is often skittish, scruffy-looking and has no branding. Look for it in large, remote wild areas and public lands.

Habitat: semideserts, shrublands, valleys

Home: no den or nest; rests in open terrain, does not seek shelter to give birth or escape bad weather

Food: herbivore; grasses and other green plants, shrubs and other woody plants

Sounds: typical horse whinnies, nickers, squeals, neighs, and snorts

Breeding: Jun–Aug mating; 11 months gestation

Young: 1 colt every other year in May or June; can walk within minutes of birth, nurses for several weeks

flehmening

mother and colt

Signs: oval depressions in grass are evidence of beds; scat in piles of large patties, several males will use a common defecation site, resulting in a large formation called a stud pile; large amounts of urine, sometimes pooling on flat open ground

Activity: diurnal; feeds for up to several hours, rests for up to 2 hours, then feeds again, may take a break at midday

Tracks: front and hind hooves 3–5" (7.5–13 cm) wide, each a large single semicircle; wide space between each print; hind hooves do not register in fore prints

Stan's Notes: Horses were domesticated over 5,000 years ago in the Old World and have been introduced all over the world. The Feral Horse, sometimes known as Wild Horse, has a wide variety of colors and patterns. While often a bit smaller than domestic horses, from a distance it is nearly impossible to differentiate wild and domestic horses from each other when they are grazing on public lands.

Diet is 90 percent grass, so the Feral won't be seen far from open grass habitat. Also needs to be near freestanding water. Typically visits a local watering hole at least daily, often in late afternoon.

Social structure is complex. Usually seen in small herds of mostly adult females (mares), their young (colts), and a dominant male (stallion). Individuals seen on their own are usually injured or young stallions who have yet to establish themselves in a herd.

Young stallions are forced out of their herds at age 3 and form small bachelor herds, led by a dominant stallion. Fights between stallions start with threat postures and displays such as laying the ears back, opening the mouth, arching the neck, and shaking the head. Physical fights include biting and kicking, often resulting in serious injury.

Takes a dust bath by rolling in exposed soils. Mutual grooming is a daily activity, although a stallion does not groom or allow itself to be groomed.

male

Fallow Deer
Dama dama

Family: Deer (Cervidae)

Size: L 4½–5½' (1.4–1.7 m); T 8–15" (20–38 cm); H 3–3½' (0.9–1.1 m)

Weight: M 175–225 lb. (79–101 kg); F 75–100 lb. (34–45 kg)

Description: Highly variable, with several forms. Rusty red to tan with white spots on back and sides merging into a line. May have a narrow black stripe along the back. White belly and legs. Small head and ears. Male has large, broad flattened (palmate) antlers with many tines; young males have spike antlers. Male gets darker and spots fade during winter. Female is smaller and lacks antlers. Both sexes have a prominent larynx (Adam's apple).

Origin/Age: non-native; 5–15 years

Compare: Mule Deer (pg. 359) lacks white spots. Sika Deer (pg. 347) has a white rump; male has a hairy mane. Look for the Adam's apple to help identify.

Habitat: grasslands, open meadows, ranches

Home: no den or nest; sleeps in a different spot every night, beds may be concentrated in one area, does not use a shelter in bad weather or winter

Food: herbivore; grasses, other green plants in summer, browse in winter includes oak and hackberry

Sounds: male gives a deep bellow and belching during rut, female bleats

Breeding: Sep–Nov mating; 7–8 months gestation

Young: 1 fawn (sometimes 2) once per year in May or June; walks within hours of birth

white male

white female

tan female

spotted female

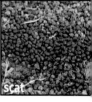

scat

Signs: grass or other green plants cut off low to the ground, beds or flattened areas in the grass indicating resting or sleeping, often under trees

Activity: nocturnal, crepuscular; most active in early morning and again at the end of daylight

Tracks: front hoof 2½–3½" (6–9 cm) long, hind hoof slightly smaller, both with a split heart shape with the point in the front; neat line of single tracks; hind hooves fall near or directly onto fore prints (direct register) when walking

Stan's Notes: A handsome medium-sized deer, highly variable in color, with several color morphs in Texas: rust, tan, white, and black, the most common being rust with spots. Darker varieties usually hide the spots and stripes. Various color morphs can be seen in one herd. Both sexes are lighter colored in summer and darker during winter. The darker winter coat often diminishes or hides the white spots.

The Fallow Deer has a long association with people, dating back to before recorded history. The Romans introduced it to central Europe and it was further introduced from Europe and Asia. It is the most widely kept deer all over the world for hunting and as food. Many escaped into the wild and are thriving. Texas has more than 10,000 individuals on private ranches for hunting purposes, with several small herds occurring in the wild. Often tame and kept as semi-domesticated animals in parks and zoos.

The genus and species name *Dama* is Latin and used for roe deer, gazelles, and antelopes. Adult males (bucks) display a moose-like flattened (palmate) antler. Only bucks have antlers, with young males growing and casting thin narrow antlers each season. After 3–4 years of age the males start to grow palmate antlers with many small tines. These antlers become very large at about ages 6–7 and look out of place compared with the body. The antlers start to decline in size from this point on.

male

Sika Deer

Cervus nippon

Family: Deer (Cervidae)

Size: L 4½–6' (1.4–1.8 m); T 6–12" (15–30 cm); H 3–3½' (0.9–1.1 m)

Weight: M 125–175 lb. (56–79 kg); F 75–125 lb. (34–56 kg)

Description: Highly variable size and color in Texas. Reddish brown to tan in summer with many white spots and a dark line running down the back onto the rump. Dark brown to nearly black in winter and lacks spots. Most have a distinctive white rump patch. Male has a thick neck mane when in rut. Male has thin antlers with 3–4 tines branching from a main beam. Female has a pair of black bumps on the forehead instead of antlers.

Origin/Age: non-native; 10–20 years

Compare: The Mule Deer (pg. 359) and White-tailed Deer (pg. 355) lack white spots in summer. Axis Deer (pg. 351) lacks the black line along its back.

Habitat: woodlands, open meadows, ranches

Home: no den or nest; sleeps in a different spot every night, beds may be concentrated in one area, does not use a shelter in bad weather or winter

Food: herbivore; grasses and green leaves of other plants in summer, woody browse in winter including oak and hackberry

Sounds: male gives a high-pitched whistle, also heehaws

Breeding: May–Aug mating; 7–8 months gestation

Young: 1 fawn once per year in January to April; walks within hours of birth, has reddish brown fur with white spots

347

females

Signs: grass or other green plants cut off low to the ground, beds or flattened areas in the grass indicating resting or sleeping, often under trees

Activity: nocturnal, crepuscular; most active in early morning and again at the end of daylight, active into the night for a couple hours

Tracks: front hoof 2–2½" (5–6 cm) long, hind hoof slightly smaller, both with a split heart shape with the point in the front; neat line of tracks; hind hooves fall near or directly onto fore prints (direct register) when walking

Stan's Notes: A small to medium deer with a small head. Highly variable in size and color. The Sika Deer ranges from reddish brown to tan and is spotted with white in the summer months. During winter it lacks spots and has a dark heavy coat. Most have a distinctive white rump patch that, regardless of the season, is especially noticeable when the deer is excited.

Originally from Siberia, Manchuria, northern China, Taiwan, and Japan, it was introduced to the United States and other countries around the world such as Australia, Denmark, Germany, Britain, France, Ireland, and New Zealand. In Texas it was imported as a game species on private ranches. The Sika Deer is closely related to the Red Deer of central Asia and the Elk (pg. 363).

Seen as one of the most elusive game species. Some of its survival strategies are unique for deer. Uses its coloring and spots to hide and camouflage, laying down when danger threatens as opposed to running away, which is typical in other species of deer. Some believe the Sika is more clever and wary than other deer, making it more sporting to hunt.

There are many subspecies of Sika Deer. It is thought that several were brought unknowingly into the United States, resulting in many hybrids. Almost all Sika Deer in Texas are behind fences on managed ranches, and about 12 counties have free-ranging populations. The total statewide population is under 10,000, with fewer than half in the wild.

Males keep territories and herd harems of females during the rut. Territory size ranges from 3–5 acres (1.2–2 ha). Territories are marked with scrapes in the ground where the male urinates and leaves a strong musky odor. Males spar, sometimes for long periods, usually not resulting in death, but injuries do occur.

male

Axis Deer

Axis axis

Family: Deer (Cervidae)

Size: L 5–6' (1.5–1.8 m); T 6–12" (15–30 cm); H 3–4' (0.9–1.2 m)

Weight: M 65–175 lb. (29–79 kg); F 55–100 lb. (25–45 kg)

Description: Yellowish brown to reddish brown dappled with small white spots. White belly, rump, throat, and inside of legs and ears, with relatively small ears. Black nose and tip of muzzle. Male has long thin antlers; each antler has 3 tines, with the lowest (brow tine) much longer than the others. Female is smaller, lighter brown and lacks antlers.

Origin/Age: non-native; 5–15 years

Compare: Mule Deer (pg. 359) is larger, lacks the white spots and bucks have larger antlers. Sika Deer (pg. 347) has a distinctive small head, hairy mane, and white rump. Fallow Deer (pg. 343) shares similar white spots, but is darker colored and bucks have distinctive flattened antlers.

Habitat: woodlands, near water, grasslands, ranches

Home: no den or nest; sleeps in a different spot every night, beds may be concentrated in one area, does not use a shelter in bad weather or winter

Food: herbivore; grasses, sedges, and other green plants; browse includes oak, hackberry, and sumac

Sounds: male gives a bugling bellow similar to elk, alarm calls given by both sexes sound like barks

Breeding: year-round mating; 7–8 months gestation

Young: 1 fawn once per year, usually January through April; walks within hours of birth

mother and young | female

Signs: grass or sedge cut off low to the ground, beds or flattened areas in the grass indicating resting or sleeping, often seeks the shelter of shade near water, avoids rugged habitat

Activity: nocturnal, crepuscular; most active in early morning and again at the end of daylight

Tracks: front hoof 2–3" (5–7.5 cm) long, hind hoof slightly smaller, both with a split heart shape with the point in the front; neat line of single tracks; hind hooves fall near or directly onto fore prints (direct register) when walking

Stan's Notes: This is a fairly large and unique-looking spotted deer. Native to India, where it is called Chital, the Axis Deer was introduced to Texas in the early 1930s. Now living in southern and central parts of Texas, it is estimated that more than 15,000 individuals are free-roaming in the state. Most likely it is the most abundant exotic deer in Texas, living in large herds from 10–100 or more individuals. Each herd has a leader, usually an experienced female (doe). Unlike our native White-tailed Deer (pg. 355), adult male (buck) Axis Deer live in herds of young and old animals of both sexes.

Axis Deer are more closely related to our Elk (pg. 363) than the White-tailed Deer or Mule Deer (pg. 359). Similar to the Elk, the Axis Deer gives a bugle-like call when mating. Unlike other deer, Axis bucks are capable of mating any time of year as long as their antlers are hardened and they are rutting. Each buck seems to be on a time schedule that is not synchronized with the other bucks. However, most rutting takes place in summer.

Does can give birth at any time of year, but seem to deliver more often from January to early April. Young (fawns) are eating green forage at 5–6 weeks of age and are completely weaned from their mother's milk at 4 months. Young females are capable of mating in their first year, but usually don't breed until they are 2 years old. Males mature and are mating by 4–5 years of age.

male

White-tailed Deer
Odocoileus virginianus

Family: Deer (Cervidae)

Size: L 4–7' (1.2–2.1 m); T 6–12" (15–30 cm); H 3–4' (0.9–1.2 m)

Weight: M 100–300 lb. (45–135 kg); F 75–200 lb. (34–90 kg)

Description: Reddish brown during summer, grayish brown during winter. Large ears, white inside with black edges. A white eye-ring, nose band, chin, throat, and belly. Brown tail with a black tip and white underside. Male has antlers with many small tines originating from a central beam and an antler spread of 12–36" (30–91 cm). Female is overall smaller, has a thinner neck, and lacks antlers.

Origin/Age: native; 5–10 years

Compare: Mule Deer (pg. 359) has a black-tipped white tail and forked tines from the main beam. Sika Deer (pg. 347) is darker brown, has a small head and short ears and antlers. Fallow Deer (pg. 343) has white spots and distinctive flattened antlers. Axis Deer (pg. 351) has white spots over its body.

Habitat: many habitats, woodlands, scrublands, ranches

Home: no den or nest; sleeps in a different spot every night, beds may be concentrated in one area, does not use a shelter in bad weather

Food: herbivore; grasses and other green plants, acorns, and nuts in summer, twigs and buds in winter

Sounds: loud whistle-like snorts, male grunts, fawn bleats

Breeding: late Oct–Nov mating; 6–7 months gestation

Young: 1–2 fawns once per year in May or June; covered with white spots, walks within hours of birth

young male

tree rub

female

scat

Signs: browsed twigs that are ripped or torn (due to the lack of upper incisor teeth), tree rubs (saplings scraped or stripped of bark) made by male while polishing antlers during the rut, oval depressions in grass or leaves are evidence of beds; round hard brown pellets during winter, segmented cylindrical masses of scat in spring and summer

Activity: nocturnal, crepuscular; moves along same trails to visit feeding areas, most active in early morning and the end of day

Tracks: front hoof 2–3" (5–7.5 cm) long, hind hoof slightly smaller, both with a split heart shape with the point in the front; neat line of single tracks; hind hooves fall near or directly onto fore prints (direct register) when walking

Stan's Notes: Many subspecies of White-tailed Deer in Texas, all appearing similar, all acting the same. More common than Mule Deer (pg. 359), which usually do not occupy the same habitats.

fawn

In summer, antlers are covered with a furry skin called velvet. Velvet contains a network of blood vessels that supplies nutrients to growing antlers. New antler growth begins after the male (buck) drops his antlers in January or February. Some females (does) grow antlers. Antler growth is tied to available nutrition. It is impossible to judge the age of a buck by the number of antler tines or antler size due to the direct correlation between antlers and nutrition. Examining teeth is a better way to estimate age.

Grows much longer guard hairs in winter, giving the animal a larger appearance than in summer. Individual hairs of the winter coat are thick and hollow and provide excellent insulation.

Usually restricts its movement to a relatively small home range and is dependent on the location of the food supply. Eats 5–9 pounds (2.3–4.1 kg) of food per day, preferring acorns in fall and fresh grass in spring. Research shows that Whitetails eat up to 500 different plants. Its four-chambered stomach enables the animal to get nutrients from poor food sources, such as twigs, and eat and drink substances that are unsuitable for people.

Able to run up to 37 mph (60 km/h), jump up to 8½ feet (2.6 m) high and leap 30 feet (9.1 m). Also an excellent swimmer.

The buck is solitary in spring and early summer, but seeks other bucks in late summer and early fall to spar. Bucks are polygamous. The largest, most dominant bucks mate with many does.

For a couple weeks after birth, fawns lay still all day while their mother is away feeding. Mother nurses them evenings and nights.

male

Mule Deer
Odocoileus hemionus

Family: Deer (Cervidae)

Size: L 4–7½' (1.2–2.3 m); T 4–9" (10–23 cm); H 3½–4' (1.1–1.2 m)

Weight: M 100–475 lb. (45–214 kg); F 75–160 lb. (34–72 kg)

Description: Reddish brown in summer. Gray in winter. White chin, throat and rump. Large ears, white inside with black tips and edges. A thin white tail with a black tip. Male has large antlers with 2 main beams, many tines and an antler spread of 2–4' (61–122 cm). Female is 20 percent smaller than male, has a thinner neck and lacks antlers.

Origin/Age: native; 10–15 years

Compare: Larger, stockier and less common than White-tailed Deer (pg. 355), which has a larger, wider tail. Antlers on White-tailed Deer have just 1 main beam. Mule Deer runs with its tail down, while the White-tailed Deer runs with its tail raised and waving back and forth.

Habitat: grasslands, semideserts, scrublands, forests

Home: no den or nest; doesn't use shelter in bad weather or winter, sleeps in dense cover each night

Food: herbivore; grasses and other green plants, acorns, and nuts in summer, twigs and buds in winter

Sounds: generally quiet; male will grunt, fawn will bleat to call its mother

Breeding: late Nov–Dec mating; 6–7 months gestation

Young: 1–2 fawns once per year in May or June; covered with white spots, walks within hours of birth

young male

fawn

female

scat

Signs: ripped or torn browsed twigs (due to the lack of upper incisor teeth), oval depressions in grass or leaves are evidence of beds; segmented cylindrical masses of scat in spring and summer, round hard brown pellets during winter

Activity: nocturnal, crepuscular; will wander about seeking feeding areas with grass

Tracks: front hoof 2½–3¼" (6–8 cm) long, hind hoof slightly smaller, both with a split heart shape with the point in the front; neat line of single tracks; hind hooves fall near or directly onto fore prints (direct register) when walking, fore hooves fall in front of hind prints when bounding in a distinctive gait (stotting)

Stan's Notes: The range of Mule Deer in the Trans-Pecos region has declined over the past 100 years. Populations in the Texas panhandle, however, seem to be on the increase.

Also called Black-tailed Deer for its black-tipped tail. Common name "Mule" comes from its large mule-like ears, which can move independently to focus on sounds originating from two different directions simultaneously. Although the ears appear substantially larger than those of White-tailed Deer (pg. 355), measurements confirm that they are about the same in both species.

Mule Deer have a unique, stiff-legged bounding gait called stotting, in which the front and hind legs move in the same fashion at the same time. Stotting helps to positively identify this animal since White-tailed Deer do not do this.

The male (buck) drops its antlers in January or February, with new growth beginning immediately. Growing antlers are covered with a velvety covering that contains a network of blood vessels. Each successive set of antlers gets larger until a buck reaches peak maturity at 6–7 years. Antlers grown after that age range have an irregular growth pattern, resulting in atypically shaped antlers. Antler growth is also affected by the amount and quality of food available. Bucks are solitary until just before the rut, when several may come together to look for females (does). Sparring between bucks is common. The objective is to overpower the opponent, and injury rarely results. Highly polygamous, a dominant buck will mate with nearly all does in his area.

Does remain in small to large groups year-round. A doe may mate with more than one buck per season. Younger does will produce single fawns, while older does produce twins annually. Fawns remain hidden in tall vegetation for their first month. Mothers visit their young each evening to nurse.

male

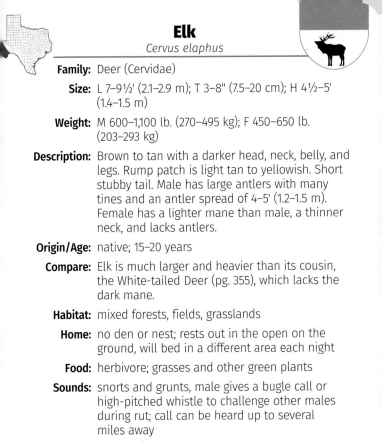

Elk
Cervus elaphus

Family: Deer (Cervidae)

Size: L 7–9½' (2.1–2.9 m); T 3–8" (7.5–20 cm); H 4½–5' (1.4–1.5 m)

Weight: M 600–1,100 lb. (270–495 kg); F 450–650 lb. (203–293 kg)

Description: Brown to tan with a darker head, neck, belly, and legs. Rump patch is light tan to yellowish. Short stubby tail. Male has large antlers with many tines and an antler spread of 4–5' (1.2–1.5 m). Female has a lighter mane than male, a thinner neck, and lacks antlers.

Origin/Age: native; 15–20 years

Compare: Elk is much larger and heavier than its cousin, the White-tailed Deer (pg. 355), which lacks the dark mane.

Habitat: mixed forests, fields, grasslands

Home: no den or nest; rests out in the open on the ground, will bed in a different area each night

Food: herbivore; grasses and other green plants

Sounds: snorts and grunts, male gives a bugle call or high-pitched whistle to challenge other males during rut; call can be heard up to several miles away

Breeding: late Aug–Nov mating; 9 months gestation

Young: 1–2 calves once per year in June or July; covered with spots until about 3 months, feeds solely by nursing for the first 30 days, weaned at 9 months

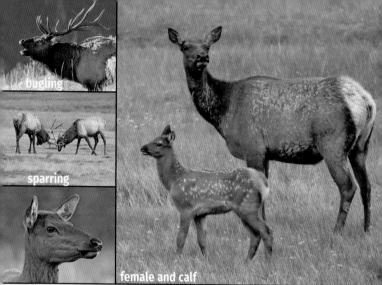

bugling

sparring

female and calf

summer scat

winter scat

Signs: tree rubs (saplings scraped or stripped of bark) made by the male while polishing antlers during rut, ground scrapes (shallow depressions in the ground) made by male hooves to attract females and where male urinates and defecates, shallow depressions in grass made from resting

Activity: nocturnal, crepuscular; can be seen during the day walking and feeding

Tracks: front hoof 4–4½" (10–11 cm) long, hind hoof slightly smaller, both with a split heart shape with the point in the front; line of individual tracks; hind hooves fall near or onto fore prints (direct register) when walking, often obliterating the front hoof tracks; heart shape widens and 2 dots (made by dewclaws) print just behind each heart-shaped print when in mud

Stan's Notes: There is only one species of elk in North America, but there are four subspecies. Sometimes called Wapiti, which is a Shawnee word meaning "pale deer." The British name for the moose is "Elk." This name apparently was misapplied by our early settlers and has remained since.

Once widespread in the western United States, with numbers at about 10 million before European settlement. Almost disappeared, dwindling down to 500–600 individuals by the early 1900s due to overhunting, and extirpated from Texas. All elk in the state today are the result of reintroduction. Reintroduced to the Guadalupe Mountains in 1928 and later to the Trans-Pecos area. Now occurs in small herds scattered across several mountain ranges.

A highly gregarious animal. Most herds consist of many females (cows) and calves. Highly territorial, marking the edges of its area with a scent secreted from glands on the sides of its chin and muzzle. Makes a shallow, saucer-like depression in dirt (wallow) in which it rolls, coating its fur with dust to help protect against annoying insects. It is a fast animal, with males (bulls) capable of reaching 35 mph (56 km/h) for short distances. Also a strong swimmer that will wade across nearly any river or stream.

A bull is solitary or found in small groups, but will join the herd during the rut. Bulls are capable of breeding at 2 years. However, rarely is a bull large enough at that age to fight off older males and establish a harem. Will thrash small trees to polish its antlers. Tears up vegetation and wears it on antlers to express dominance. Top bulls challenge each other by clashing their antlers together in a jousting fashion. Rarely do these fights result in any injury or death. The most polygamous animal in the United States, one bull will mate with all cows in the harem.

The cow becomes sexually mature at 3 years. A cow will leave the herd to give birth, rejoining the group 4–10 days later.

Feral Pig
Sus scrofa

Family: Old World Swine (Suidae)

Size: L 4–6' (1.2–1.8 m); T 6–12" (15–30 cm); H 2–3' (61–91 cm)

Weight: M 200–400 lb. (90–180 kg); F 75–300 lb. (34–135 kg)

Description: Extremely variable in color from dark brown and black to gray and white. Large thick body, long pointed snout and short dark legs. Thick fur and well-furred ears. Tail is furred and hangs straight down. Tusks up to 9" (23 cm) long, curling out alongside of mouth. Tiny dark eyes. Female has the same colors, but is smaller and lacks tusks.

Origin/Age: non-native; 15–20 years

Compare: Larger than Javelina (pg. 307), which has short straight tusks and a narrow white collar across its shoulders.

Habitat: open forests, shrublands, semideserts

Home: no den or nest, rests out in the open or in open forests; female does not seek shelter to give birth, but makes a bed for birthing not far from water

Food: omnivore; grasses and other green plants, insects, mammals, reptiles, amphibians, birds

Sounds: snorts and grunts similar to domestic pigs

Breeding: year-round mating; 16 weeks gestation

Young: 5–7 piglets twice per year; only 6–8" (15–20 cm) at birth, usually brown with pale longitudinal body stripes, able to walk and follow mother at 1 week, nurses for 3 months

Signs: large holes in the ground where plants, crops, fences, posts, or other objects were uprooted, mud wallowing holes; mass of pellets or tubular segments, usually near uprooted plants

Activity: diurnal, nocturnal, crepuscular; feeds for up to several hours, sits down to rest for up to 2 hours, then feeds again

Tracks: front hoof 2½–3" (6–7.5 cm) long, hind hoof slightly smaller, widely split at the front with a point in front; neat line of paired tracks, slightly offset; hind hooves fall near fore prints (no direct register) when walking

Stan's Notes: Most feral pigs are descendants of European wild hogs that were introduced into the United States for food or for sporting purposes. Some are the progeny of escaped domestic swine that became feral over just a couple generations. Feral Pigs and domestic hogs can and do interbreed, producing traits of both species such as a cartilaginous, flexible snout. Now found in over half of the United States, mainly in the South, with range expanding northward.

Feral Pigs prefer forests that produce acorn crops, but in absence of this they will live in open shrublands and other areas not far from water. Their presence has a noticeable impact on native wildlife and plant life, as well as on crops and livestock, and for this reason the animals are not welcome in many places. Other areas, however, embrace their presence with managed hunting. It is estimated that more than 1 million Feral Pigs live in Texas. By pushing out native species such as the Javelina (pg. 307), they represent one of the most serious conservation threats.

Also called Razorback, Russian Wild Boar, Wild Boar, and Wild Hog. A female (sow) and her young (piglets) will feed together and sometimes join other groups in herds of up to 35 individuals. The male (boar) tends to be solitary unless it is breeding season. Boars will fight, using their tusks to determine dominance and the right to breed.

Piglets stay with their mother for a year. They are usually brown with pale longitudinal body stripes at birth, and become sexually mature at just 18 months of age.

Black Bear
Ursus americanus

Family: Bears (Ursidae)

Size: L 4½–6' (1.4–1.8 m); T 3–7" (7.5–18 cm); H 3–3½' (0.9–1.1 m)

Weight: M 100–900 lb. (45–405 kg); F 90–525 lb. (41–236 kg)

Description: Nearly all black, sometimes brown, tan, or cinnamon. Short round ears. Light brown snout. May have a small white patch on its chest. Short tail, which often goes unnoticed.

Origin/Age: native; 15–30 years

Compare: The only bear species in Texas.

Habitat: all forest types, grasslands

Home: den, underneath a fallen tree or in a rock crevice or cave, may dig a den 5–6' (1.5–1.8 m) deep with a small cavity at the end; male sometimes hibernates on the ground without shelter

Food: omnivore; leaves, nuts, roots, fruit, berries, grass, insects, fish, small mammals, carrion

Sounds: huffs, puffs, or grunts and groans when walking, loud snorts made by air forced from nostrils, loud roars when fighting and occasionally when mating, motor-like humming when content

Breeding: Jun–Jul mating; 60–90 days gestation; implantation delayed until November after mating

Young: 1–5 (usually 2) cubs every other year in January or February; born covered with fine dark fur, weighing only ½–1 lb. (0.2–0.5 kg)

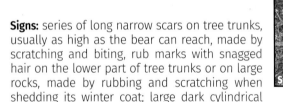

claw marks   brown morph

scat

Signs: series of long narrow scars on tree trunks, usually as high as the bear can reach, made by scratching and biting, rub marks with snagged hair on the lower part of tree trunks or on large rocks, made by rubbing and scratching when shedding its winter coat; large dark cylindrical scat or piles of loose scat, usually contains berries and nuts, may contain animal hair, undigested plant stems, and roots

Activity: diurnal, nocturnal; often seen feeding during the day

Tracks: hind paw 7–9" (18–23 cm) long, 5" (13 cm) wide with 5 toes, turns inward slightly, looks like a human footprint, forepaw 4" (10 cm) long, 5" (13 cm) wide with 5 toes, claw marks on all feet; fore and hind prints are parallel, hind paws fall several inches in front of fore prints; shuffles feet when walking

Stan's Notes: The Black Bear is unique to North America. Has a shuffling gait and frequently appears clumsy. It is not designed for speed, but can run up to 30 mph (48 km/h) for short distances. A powerful swimmer, however, and good at climbing trees. It has color vision, but poor eyesight and relies on smell to find most of its food. Often alone except for mating in early summer or when bears gather at a large food supply such as a garbage dump. Feeds heavily throughout summer, adding layers of fat for hibernation.

In northern parts of its range it hibernates up to five months per year starting in late fall. In Texas it appears to hibernate for a much shorter time, and occasionally wakes and moves around the den in winter. Heart rate drops from 70 to 10–20 beats per minute. Body temperature drops only 1–12°F (–17°C to –11°C), which is not enough to change mental functions. Doesn't eat, drink, pass feces, or urinate during hibernation despite rousing. A female can lose up to 40 percent of its body weight during hibernation.

cub

A male has a large territory up to 15 square miles (39 sq. km) that often encompasses several female territories. Males fight each other for breeding rights and usually have scars from fights. Male bears mature at 3–4 years, but don't become full size until 10–12 years. They do not help to raise the young.

Females don't breed until 2–3 years of age. A female with more body fat when entering hibernation will have more cubs than others with less fat. If a female lacks enough fat, she won't give birth. Mothers average 177 pounds (80 kg)— about 250 times the size of newborns. A short gestation and tiny cubs are the result of the reproductive process during hibernation.

Once considered extinct in Texas. In recent history, bears from Mexico have repopulated the state and are now doing better.

Atlantic Spotted Dolphin
Stenella frontalis

Family: Marine Dolphins (Delphinidae)

Size: L 6–6½' (1.8–2 m)

Weight: 250–275 lb. (113–124 kg)

Description: Smooth purplish gray body covered with white spots, especially on the sides. Nearly white belly. Often appears black from a distance. Short stocky snout (beak). Small round eyes on sides of head just behind the line of the jaw. Breathing hole on top of head behind eyes. Large fin on the back (dorsal) curves back and points toward the tail (falcate). Short, thick powerful tail. Long flippers. Some individuals have more spots than others. Male is longer and heavier than the female.

Origin/Age: native to Gulf waters off the coast of Texas and the entire Atlantic Ocean; 20–25 years

Compare: Smaller than the Bottlenose Dolphin (pg. 379), which has shorter flippers and lacks white spots. The much larger Sperm Whale (pg. 383) has a huge body and lacks a well-defined beak.

Habitat: open seas, deeper bays, inlets

Home: roams open waters with no well-defined territory, often following seasonal patterns; rests in open water near coral reefs

Food: ichthyophagous; fish, squid, invertebrates

Sounds: series of squeaks, whistles, chirps, growls, barks, and chuckles above and below water

Breeding: Jun–Aug mating; 12 months gestation

Young: 1 calf every 2–3 years; born swimming, nurses for up to 1 year

Signs: shadows of large individuals swimming in groups of up to 50 individuals, riding bow waves of boats, feeding around fishing and shrimp boats, individuals breaking the surface of the water, leaping into the air or surfacing for air just offshore

Activity: diurnal, nocturnal; active year-round

Tracks: none

Stan's Notes: A small dolphin, often appearing very dark from a distance. Shows a large number of small white spots when seen up close. A congregation of spots results in a blaze or white stripe on the side. Amount of spots is highly variable among individuals.

Less common than the Bottlenose Dolphin (pg. 379). Doesn't do well in captivity and is not as familiar to the general public as the Bottlenose. Often in groups, called pods or schools, of 10–20 dolphins; sometimes in larger groups of up to 50 individuals.

Occurring only in warm waters of the Atlantic, it is the second most common dolphin in the Gulf of Mexico. More common offshore than near shore. When near shore, it is thought to be responding to prey items heading to shallow waters.

Has a smooth, streamlined body. Adults have 60–84 teeth. Young are born in spring and summer and lack spots. All ride the bow waves of large ships and jump from the water.

The Delphinidae family has 37 species of dolphins and spouted whales, which are closely related. There have been 9 dolphin and 5 spouted whale species seen in Texas during the past 100 years or more. The eight other dolphins include the Bottlenose Dolphin, Striped Dolphin, Pantropical Spotted Dolphin, Clymene Dolphin, Rough-toothed Dolphin, Spinner Dolphin, Risso's Dolphin, and Fraser's Dolphin. Unfortunately, most of these are only known in Texas from single reports or by dead individuals washing to shore after major storms.

Bottlenose Dolphin

Tursiops truncatus

Family: Marine Dolphins (Delphinidae)

Size: L 8–8½' (2.4–2.6 m)

Weight: 450–550 lb. (203–248 kg)

Description: Smooth and streamlined gray body with a large head, short stocky snout (beak), and lighter belly. Small round eyes on the sides of head. Breathing hole on top of head behind the eyes. Large fin on the back (dorsal) curves back and points toward the tail (falcate). Short, thick powerful tail. Some individuals are darker than others. May have lighter areas of scarring from old injuries. Male is longer and heavier than the female.

Origin/Age: native to Gulf waters off the Texas coast and the Atlantic and Pacific Oceans; 20–25 years

Compare: Larger than Atlantic Spotted Dolphin (pg. 375), which is stockier and has white spotting on its sides. Sperm Whale (pg. 383) is much larger, with a huge body and small dorsal fin and lacks a well-defined beak.

Habitat: open seas, bays, inlets, saltwater lagoons

Home: some stay in 1 bay, others roam open waters with no well-defined territory, often following seasonal patterns; rests in open water near coral reefs

Food: ichthyophagous; fish, squid, invertebrates

Sounds: series of squeaks, pops, and chuckles above and below water

Breeding: Jun–Aug mating; 12 months gestation

Young: 1 calf every 2–3 years; born swimming, nurses for up to 1 year

breaching | pod

Signs: shadows of large individuals swimming in groups, riding bow waves of boats, feeding around fishing and shrimp boats, individuals breaking the surface of the water, leaping into the air (breaching) or surfacing for air just offshore

Activity: diurnal, nocturnal; active year-round

Tracks: none

Stan's Notes: A familiar marine mammal, made famous by the television show "Flipper." Now seen in many marine or aquarium displays and museums. The Bottlenose is the most widespread and common of Gulf coast dolphin and can be seen in relatively shallow water in lagoons, bays, and inlets. The majority, however, are found well out to sea. Found throughout temperate and tropical waters of the world.

Often in groups, called pods or schools, of 2–20 individuals, but can be seen in larger groups of up to 100 dolphins. Some groups are sedentary, remaining in a small territory of one bay; others are migratory. Populations tend to increase off the coast of Texas during fall and winter.

It is thought there are two distinct Bottlenose Dolphin forms in the Gulf of Mexico: inshore dolphins that inhabit shallow water and offshore populations remaining in deeper waters. Differences in body shape and fin size show that the inshore dolphins are adapting to shallower water.

Dolphins eat a wide variety of food depending on the abundance at the time. They eat mainly fish including shark, tarpon, pike, rays, mullet, catfish and anchovies, along with eels. A dolphin can eat 40–50 pounds (18–23 kg) of food daily. Individuals of a group often work together when feeding. Sometimes several dolphins will herd fish into tight schools while others wait at the bottom and swim up to feed. Other times dolphins may simply chase fish into shallow water, where they lunge for their prey.

Sperm Whale
Physeter macrocephalus

Family: Sperm Whale (Physeteridae)

Size: M 50–65' (15–20 m); F 35–45' (10.7–13.7 m)

Weight: M 30–35 tons (27.2–31.8 mt); F 12–15 tons (10.9–37.6 mt)

Description: Extremely large, gray to nearly black with a huge square head and blunt nose. Small round eyes on the sides of head, far back behind the angle of the jaw. Long slit mouth with white lips under the head. Breathing hole on top of head in front of eyes. Tiny round fin on the back (dorsal), closer to the tail than the head. Massive powerful tail, often with a distinctive color pattern or markings. Male is much longer and heavier than female.

Origin/Age: native to Gulf waters off the coast of Texas and all oceans worldwide; 50–100 years

Compare: The largest and most common whale in the Gulf of Mexico. Look for its massive square head when it surfaces and tail flipping (fluking) as it dives.

Habitat: open seas, deep waters

Home: waters off the coast of Texas year-round, roams oceans all around the world

Food: ichthyophagous; deep-water squid, occasionally other deep-water prey including octopi, lobsters, jellyfish, crabs, sponges and some fish

Sounds: series of clicks and pops, produced in a sequence called a coda

Breeding: any time of year; 15 months gestation

Young: 1 calf every 5–7 years; born swimming, nurses for up to 2 years

383

fluking spouting

Signs: shadows of enormous individuals swimming in deep waters, hump on the back and dorsal fin rising above the surface, individuals surfacing to breathe (spouting), jumping out of the water (breaching) and flipping their tails into the air before submerging (fluking)

Activity: diurnal, nocturnal; active year-round

Tracks: none

Stan's Notes: The largest toothed animal and marine mammal, roaming oceans and seas around the world except for the polar ice fields. One of nearly 20 marine mammal species with the common name "Whale," it is the only member of its family, Physeteridae.

Was hunted by nearly all nations for its waxy oil. Produced by the spermaceti organ, a Sperm Whale can hold up to 500 gallons (1,895 L) of oil in its massive head. With widespread use of the oil in lubricants, lamps, candles, and perfumes, the species was the mainstay of the whaling industry until hunting was banned internationally in the 1970s due to dwindling populations.

Dives deeper than 9,500 feet (2,895 m), where it hunts for giant deep-water squid, its main diet. Up to 1 ton (0.9 mt) of squid daily is needed to sustain an adult male.

Highly sexually dimorphic, males can be twice the weight and size of females. Adult males are highly migratory and solitary. They tend to be loners except when attending a harem of females for breeding. Females remain in groups all year and congregate in tropical or subtropical waters. Males move to warmer waters in winter, where they find the females.

Female Sperm Whales have different breeding cycles from each other due to their age and whether or not they have a calf. Males follow groups, called pods or schools, of females and guard them from other males until a female is ready to breed. Many females in a harem may already be pregnant or tending young, making only few available, even in large harems of 30 individuals. It can take up to 7 years for a female to be ready to mate again.

Other whales in Texas have been seen only rarely, usually when a dead specimen has beached after a large storm. These include the Killer Whale, False Killer Whale, Pygmy Killer Whale, Melon-headed Whale, Short-finned Pilot Whale, Northern Right Whale and Minke Whale.

GLOSSARY

Browse: Twigs, buds, leaves, and other parts of woody plants eaten by deer, elk, and other animals

Canid: A member of the Wolves, Foxes, and Coyote family, which includes dogs.

Carnivore: An animal, such as a mink, fox, or wolf, that eats the flesh of other animals for its main nutrition.

Carrion: Dead or decaying flesh. Carrion is a significant food source for many animal species.

Cecum: The large pouch that forms the beginning of the large intestine. Also known as the blind gut.

Cheek ruff: A gathering of long stiff hairs on each side of the face of an animal, ending in a downward point. Seen in bobcats.

Coprophagy: The act of reingesting fecal pellets. Coprophagy enables rabbits and hares to gain more nourishment since the pellets pass through the digestive system a second time.

Crepuscular: Active during the early morning and late evening hours as opposed to day or night. See *diurnal* and *nocturnal*.

Cud: Food regurgitated from the first stomach to the mouth, and chewed again. Cud is produced by hoofed animals such as deer or bison; these animals have a four-chambered stomach and are known as ruminants.

Dewclaw: A nonfunctional (vestigial) digit on the feet of some animals, which does not touch the ground. Seen in deer and elk.

Direct register: The act of a hind paw landing or registering in the track left by a forepaw, resulting in two prints that appear like one track. Usually occurs when walking.

Diurnal: Active during daylight hours as opposed to nighttime hours. Opposite of *nocturnal*.

Drey: The nest of a squirrel.

Duff: The layer of decaying leaves, grasses, twigs, or branches, often several inches thick, on a forest floor or prairie.

Echolocation: A sensory system in bats, dolphins, and some shrews, in which inaudible, high-pitched sounds are emitted and the returning echoes are interpreted to determine the direction and distance of objects such as prey.

Estrus: A state of sexual readiness in most female animals that immediately precedes ovulation, and the time when females are most receptive to mating. Also known as heat.

Extirpate: To hunt or trap into extinction in a region or state.

Flehmen: The lift of the upper lip and grimace an animal makes when it draws air into its mouth and over its Jacobson's organ, which is thought to help analyze the scents (pheromones) wafting in the air. Frequently seen in cats, deer, and bison.

Fossorial: Well suited for burrowing or digging. Describes an animal such as a mole.

Gestation: Pregnancy. The period of development in the uterus of a mammal from conception up to birth.

Grizzled: Streaked or tipped with gray, or partly gray. Describes the appearance of some fur.

Guard hairs: The long outer hairs of an animal's coat, which provide warmth. Guard hairs are typically hollow and usually thicker and darker than the soft hairs underneath.

Haul out: A well-worn trail or area on the shore where an animal, such as an otter, climbs or hauls itself out of the water.

Herbivore: An animal, such as a rabbit, deer, or elk, that eats plants for its main nutrition.

Hibernation: A torpid or lethargic state characterized by decreased heart rate, respiration, and body temperature, and occurring in close quarters for long periods during winter. See *torpor*.

Hoary: Partly white or silver streaked, or tipped with white or silver. Describes the appearance of some fur.

Hummock: A low mound or ridge of earth or plants.

Insectivore: An animal, such as a shrew, that eats insects as its main nutrition.

Keratin: A hard protein that is the chief component of the hair, nails, horns, and hooves of an animal.

Microflora: Bacterial life living in the gut or first stomach of an animal. Microflora help break down food and aid in the digestive process.

Midden: A mound or deposit of pine cone parts and other refuse. A midden is evidence of a favorite feeding site of an animal such as a squirrel.

Morph: One of various distinct shapes, structural differences, or colors of an animal. Color morphs do not change during the life of an animal.

Nictitating membrane: A second, inner eyelid, usually translucent, that protects and moistens the eye.

Nocturnal: Active during nighttime hours as opposed to daylight hours. Opposite of *diurnal*.

Nonretractile: That which cannot be drawn back or in. Describes the claws of a dog. Opposite of retractile.

Omnivore: An animal, such as a bear, that eats a wide range of foods including plants, insects, and the flesh of other animals as its main nutrition.

Patagium: A thin membrane extending from the body to the front and hind limbs, forming a wing-like extension. Seen in flying squirrels and bats.

Population: All individuals of a species within a specific area.

Predator: An animal that hunts, kills, and consumes other animals. See *prey*.

Prey: An animal that is hunted, killed, and eaten by a predator. See *predator*.

Retractile: That which can be drawn back or in. Describes the claws of a cat. Opposite of *nonretractile*.

Rut: An annually recurring condition of sexual readiness and reproductive activity in mammals, such as deer and elk, that usually occurs in autumn. See *estrus*.

Scat: The fecal droppings of an animal.

Scent marking: A means of marking territory, signaling sexual availability, or communicating an individual's identity. An animal scent marks with urine, feces, or by secreting a tiny amount of odorous liquid from a gland, usually near the base of the tail, chin, or feet, onto specific areas such as rocks, trees, and stumps.

Semifossorial: Suited for burrowing or digging. Describes an animal such as a Kit Fox.

Semiprehensile: Suited for partially seizing, grasping, or holding, especially by wrapping around an object, but not a means of full support. Describes the tail of an opossum.

Stride: In larger animals, the distance between individual tracks. In smaller animals such as weasels, the distance between sets of tracks.

Subterranean: Below the surface of the earth.

Talus: The accumulation of many rocks at the base of a cliff or mountain slope.

Tannin: A bitter-tasting astringent found in the nuts of many plant species, especially acorns.

Torpor: A torpid or lethargic state resembling hibernation, characterized by decreased heart rate, respiration, and body temperature, but usually shorter, lasting from a few hours to several days or weeks. See *hibernation*.

Tragus: A fleshy projection in the central part of the ear of most bats. The size and shape of the tragus may be used to help identify some bat species.

Tree rub: An area on small to medium trees where the bark has been scraped or stripped off. A tree rub is made by a male deer polishing his antlers in preparation for the rut.

Velvet: A soft, furry covering on antlers that contains many blood vessels, which support antler growth. Velvet is shed when antlers reach full size. Seen in the Deer family.

Vibrissae: Sensitive bristles and hairs, such as whiskers, that help an animal feel its way in the dark. Vibrissae are often on the face, legs, and tail.

Wallow: A depression in the ground that is devoid of vegetation, where an animal, such as a bison, rolls around on its back to "bathe" in dirt.

HELPFUL RESOURCES
Emergency

For an animal bite, please seek medical attention at an emergency room or call 911. Injured or orphaned animals should be turned over to a licensed wildlife rehabilitator. Check your local listings for a rehabilitator near you.

Web Pages

The internet is a valuable place to learn more about mammals. You may find studying mammals on the net a fun way to discover additional information about them or to spend a long winter night. These web sites will assist you in your pursuit of mammals. If a web address doesn't work (they often change a bit), just enter the name of the group into a search engine to track down the new web address.

Site and Address:

Smithsonian Institution - North American Mammals
naturalhistory.si.edu/research/vertebrate-zoology/mammals

The American Society of Mammalogists
www.mammalsociety.org

National Wildlife Rehabilitators Association
www.nwrawildlife.org

International Wildlife Rehabilitation Council
theiwrc.org

Texas Parks and Wildlife Department
www.tpwd.texas.gov

Author Stan Tekiela's home page
www.naturesmart.com

Texas Artiodactyla Order

ORDER	SUBORDER	FAMILY	SUBFAMILY

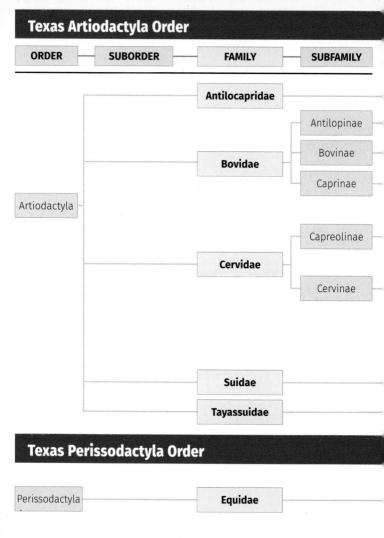

Artiodactyla

- Antilocapridae
- Bovidae
  - Antilopinae
  - Bovinae
  - Caprinae
- Cervidae
  - Capreolinae
  - Cervinae
- Suidae
- Tayassuidae

Texas Perissodactyla Order

Perissodactyla — Equidae

Even-toed Hooved Animals

Pronghorn pg. 331
Antilocapra americana

Blackbuck pg. 311
Antilope cervicapra

Nilgai pg. 315
Boselaphus tragocamelus

American Bison pg. 327
Bison bison

Barbary Sheep pg. 319
Ammotragus lervia

Bighorn Sheep pg. 323
Ovis canadensis

White-tailed Deer pg. 355
Odocoileus virginianus
Mule Deer pg. 359
Odocoileus hemionus

Fallow Deer pg. 343
Dama dama

Sika Deer pg. 347
Cervus nippon
Elk pg. 363
Cervus elaphus

Axis Deer pg. 351
Axis axis

Feral Pig pg. 367
Sus scrofa

Javelina pg. 307
Pecari tajacu

Odd-toed Hooved Animals

Burro pg. 335
Equus asinus
Feral Horse pg. 339
Equus caballus

Box colors match the
corresponding section of the book.

| ORDER | SUBORDER | FAMILY | SUBFAMILY |

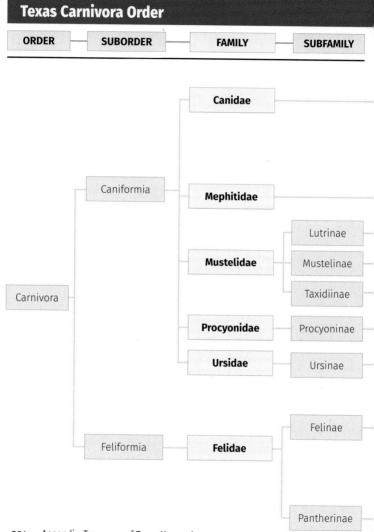

Carnivora

Caniformia

Canidae

Mephitidae

Mustelidae
- Lutrinae
- Mustelinae
- Taxidiinae

Procyonidae — Procyoninae

Ursidae — Ursinae

Feliformia — **Felidae**
- Felinae
- Pantherinae

Meat-eating Predators

Kit Fox pg. 255
Vulpes macrotis

Swift Fox pg. 259
Vulpes velox

Red Fox pg. 267
Vulpes vulpes

Gray Fox pg. 263
Urocyon cinereoargenteus

Coyote pg. 271
Canis latrans

Red Wolf pg. 275
Canis rufus

Gray Wolf pg. 279
Canis lupus

Northern River Otter pg. 207
Lontra canadensis

Long-tailed Weasel pg. 191
Mustela frenata

Mink pg. 195
Mustela vison

Black-footed Ferret pg. 199
Mustela nigripes

American Badger pg. 203
Taxidea taxus

Black Bear pg. 371
Ursus americanus

Ocelot pg. 283
Leopardus pardalis

Margay pg. 291
Leopardus wiedii

Jaguarundi pg. 287
Puma yagouaroundi

Bobcat pg. 295
Lynx rufus

Mountain Lion pg. 299
Puma concolor

Jaguar pg. 303
Panthera onca

Western Spotted Skunk pg. 211
Spilogale gracilis

Eastern Spotted Skunk pg. 219
Spilogale putorius

Hooded Skunk pg. 215
Mephitis macroura

Striped Skunk pg. 227
Mephitis mephitis

Hog-nosed Skunk pg. 223
Conepatus leuconotus

Ringtail pg. 231
Bassariscus astutus

Northern Raccoon pg. 235
Procyon lotor

White-nosed Coati pg. 239
Nasua narica

Box colors match the
corresponding section of the book.

395

Texas Cetacea Order

ORDER	SUBORDER	FAMILY	SUBFAMILY

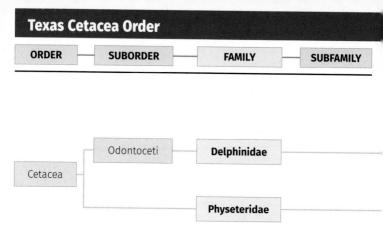

Cetacea

Odontoceti

Delphinidae

Physeteridae

Texas Cingulata Order

ORDER	SUBORDER	FAMILY	SUBFAMILY

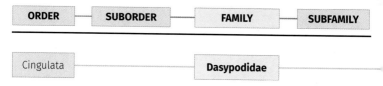

Cingulata

Dasypodidae

Dolphins and Whale

Atlantic Spotted Dolphin pg. 375
Stenella frontalis

Bottlenose Dolphin pg. 379
Tursiops truncatus

Sperm Whale pg. 383
Physeter macrocephalus

Armadillo

Nine-banded Armadillo pg. 243
Dasypus novemcinctus

Box colors match the
corresponding section of the book.

Texas Chiroptera Order

| ORDER | SUBORDER | FAMILY | SUBFAMILY |

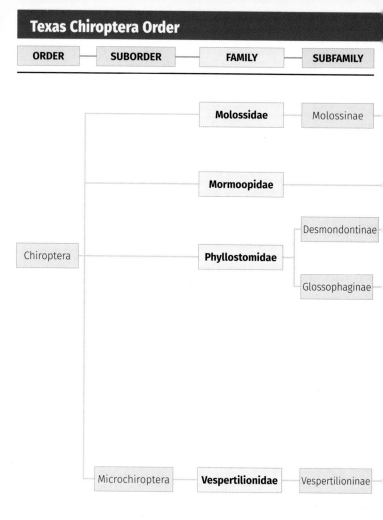

Chiroptera

Molossidae — Molossinae

Mormoopidae

Phyllostomidae — Desmondontinae

Phyllostomidae — Glossophaginae

Microchiroptera — Vespertilionidae — Vespertilioninae

Brazilian Free-tailed Bat pg. 121
Tadarida brasiliensis

Pocketed Free-tailed Bat pg. 126
Nyctinomops femorosacca
Big Free-tailed Bat pg. 127
Nyctinomops macrotis

Western Bonneted Bat pg. 127
Eumops perotis

Ghost-faced Bat pg. 125
Mormoops megalophylla

Hairy-legged Vampire Bat pg. 125
Diphylla ecaudata

Mexican Long-nosed Bat pg. 126
Leptonycteris nivalis

Mexican Long-tongued Bat pg. 126
Choeronycteris mexicana

Western Small-footed Myotis pg. 124
Myotis ciliolabrum
Fringed Myotis pg. 125
Myotis thysanodes
California Myotis pg. 125
Myotis californicus
Yuma Myotis pg. 125
Myotis yumanensis
Long-legged Myotis pg. 126
Myotis volans
Southeastern Myotis pg. 126
Myotis austroriparius
Cave Myotis pg. 126
Myotis velifer

Eastern Pipistrelle pg. 124
Pipistrellus subflavus
Western Pipistrelle pg. 125
Pipistrellus hesperus

Evening Bat pg. 124
Nycticeius humeralis

Big Brown Bat pg. 125
Eptesicus fuscus

Silver-haired Bat pg. 125
Lasionycteris noctivagans

Eastern Red Bat pg. 125
Lasiurus borealis
Hoary Bat pg. 125
Lasiurus cinereus
Western Red Bat pg. 126
Lasiurus blossevillii
Western Yellow Bat pg. 126
Lasiurus xanthinus
Northern Yellow Bat pg. 126
Lasiurus intermedius
Seminole Bat pg. 126
Lasiurus seminolus
Southern Yellow Bat pg. 127
Lasiurus ega

Townsend's Big-eared Bat pg. 125
Corynorhinus townsendii
Rafinesque's Big-eared Bat pg. 126
Corynorhinus rafinesquii

Spotted Bat pg. 125
Euderma maculatum

Pallid Bat pg. 126
Antrozous pallidus

Box colors match the
corresponding section of the book.

399

Texas Didelphimorphia Order

ORDER	SUBORDER	FAMILY	SUBFAMILY
Didelphimorphia		Didelphidae	Didelphinae

Texas Eulipotyphla Order

ORDER	SUBORDER	FAMILY	SUBFAMILY
Eulipotyphla		Soricidae	Soricinae
		Talpidae	Talpinae

Texas Lagomorpha Order

ORDER	SUBORDER	FAMILY	SUBFAMILY
Lagomorpha		Leporidae	

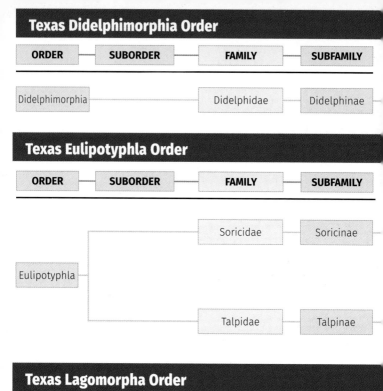

Marsupial

Virginia Opossum pg. 251
Didelphis virginiana

Shrews and Mole

Least Shrew pg. 45
Cryptotis parva

Desert Shrew pg. 49
Notiosorex crawfordi

Southern Short-tailed Shrew pg. 49
Blarina carolinensis
Elliot's Short-tailed Shrew pg. 49
Blarina hylophaga

Eastern Mole pg. 51
Scalopus aquaticus

Rabbits and Hare

Desert Cottontail pg. 175
Sylvilagus audubonii
Eastern Cottontail pg. 179
Sylvilagus floridanus
Swamp Rabbit pg. 183
Sylvilagus aquaticus

Black-tailed Jackrabbit pg. 187
Lepus californicus

Box colors match the
corresponding section of the book.

Texas Rodentia Order

ORDER	SUBORDER	FAMILY	SUBFAMILY

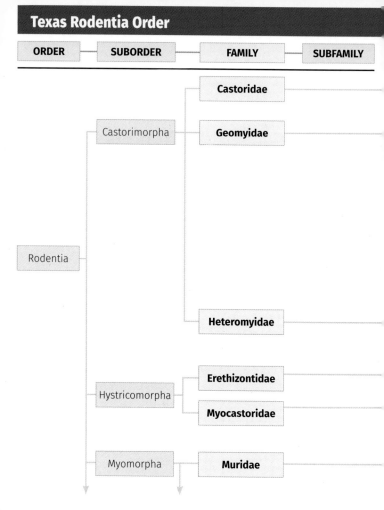

Rodentia

Castorimorpha
- **Castoridae**
- **Geomyidae**
- **Heteromyidae**

Hystricomorpha
- **Erethizontidae**
- **Myocastoridae**

Myomorpha
- **Muridae**

Continued on pages 404–407

American Beaver pg. 117
Castor canadensis

Botta's Pocket Gopher pg. 172
Thomomys bottae

Baird's Pocket Gopher pg. 172
Geomys breviceps
Desert Pocket Gopher pg. 173
Geomys arenarius
Attwater's Pocket Gopher pg. 173
Geomys attwateri
Llano Pocket Gopher pg. 173
Geomys texensis
Jones's Pocket Gopher pg. 173
Geomys knoxjonesi
Strecker's Pocket Gopher pg. 173
Geomys streckerii
Texas Pocket Gopher pg. 173
Geomys personatus
Plains Pocket Gopher pg. 169
Geomys bursarius

Yellow-faced Pocket Gopher pg. 173
Cratogeomys castanops

Merriam's Pocket Mouse pg. 70
Perognathus merriami
Silky Pocket Mouse pg. 70
Perognathus flavus
Plains Pocket Mouse pg. 71
Perognathus flavescens

Rock Pocket Mouse pg. 70
Chaetodipus intermedius
Nelson's Pocket Mouse pg. 70
Chaetodipus nelsoni
Chihuahuan Desert Pocket Mouse pg. 71
Chaetodipus eremicus
Hispid Pocket Mouse pg. 67
Chaetodipus hispidus

Mexican Spiny Pocket Mouse pg. 71
Liomys irroratus

Gulf Coast Kangaroo Rat pg. 85
Dipodomys compactus
Texas Kangaroo Rat pg. 85
Dipodomys elator
Merriam's Kangaroo Rat pg. 85
Dipodomys merriami
Ord's Kangaroo Rat pg. 81
Dipodomys ordii
Banner-tailed Kangaroo Rat pg. 85
Dipodomys spectabilis

North American Porcupine pg. 247
Erethizon dorsatum

Nutria pg. 113
Myocastor coypus

Golden Mouse pg. 65
Ochrotomys nuttalli

Box colors match the
corresponding section of the book.

| ORDER | SUBORDER | FAMILY | SUBFAMILY |

Continued from pages 402–403

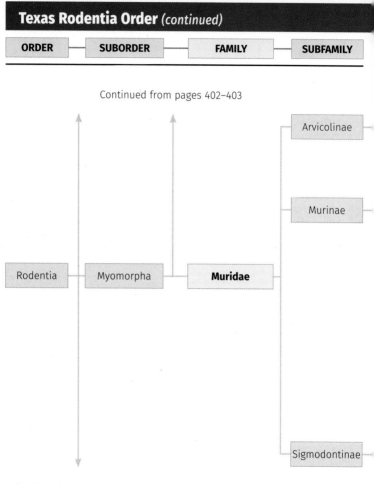

Continued on pages 406–407

Woodland Vole pg. 103
Microtus pinetorum
Prairie Vole pg. 107
Microtus ochrogaster
Mexican Vole pg. 107
Microtus mexicanus

Muskrat pg. 109
Ondatra zibethicus

House Mouse pg. 64
Mus musculus

Black Rat pg. 101
Rattus rattus
Norway Rat pg. 99
Rattus norvegicus

Northern Pygmy Mouse pg. 64
Baiomys taylori

Eastern Harvest Mouse pg. 59
Reithrodontomys humulis
Fulvous Harvest Mouse pg. 55
Reithrodontomys fulvescens
Western Harvest Mouse pg. 59
Reithrodontomys megalotis
Plains Harvest Mouse pg. 59
Reithrodontomys montanus

Mearns' Grasshopper Mouse pg. 75
Onychomys arenicola
Northern Grasshopper Mouse pg. 73
Onychomys leucogaster

White-footed Mouse pg. 61
Peromyscus leucopus
Deer Mouse pg. 64
Peromyscus maniculatus
Cactus Mouse pg. 64
Peromyscus eremicus
White-ankled Mouse pg. 65
Peromyscus pectoralis
Pinyon Mouse pg. 65
Peromyscus truei
Texas Mouse pg. 65
Peromyscus attwateri
Cotton Mouse pg. 65
Peromyscus gossypinus
Northern Rock Mouse pg. 65
Peromyscus nasutus
Brush Mouse pg. 65
Peromyscus boylii

Marsh Rice Rat pg. 77
Oryzomys palustris
Coues' Rice Rat pg. 79
Oryzomys couesi

Yellow-nosed Cotton Rat pg. 91
Sigmodon ochrognathus
Tawny-bellied Cotton Rat pg. 91
Sigmodon fulviventer
Hispid Cotton Rat pg. 87
Sigmodon hispidus

Southern Plains Woodrat pg. 93
Neotoma micropus
Eastern White-throated Woodrat pg. 97
Neotoma leucodon
Mexican Woodrat pg. 97
Neotoma mexicana
Eastern Woodrat pg. 97
Neotoma floridana

Box colors match the
corresponding section of the book.

ORDER	SUBORDER	FAMILY	SUBFAMILY

Continued from pages 402–405

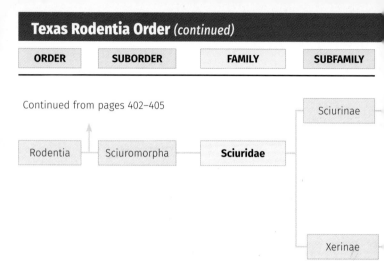

Rodentia — Sciuromorpha — **Sciuridae** — Sciurinae / Xerinae

Rodents

Southern Flying Squirrel pg. 133
Glaucomys volans

Eastern Gray Squirrel pg. 157
Sciurus carolinensis
Eastern Fox Squirrel pg. 161
Sciurus niger

Gray-footed Chipmunk pg. 129
Tamias canipes

Spotted Ground Squirrel pg. 137
Xerospermophilus spilosoma
Thirteen-lined Ground Squirrel pg. 145
Ictidomys tridecemlineatus
Mexican Ground Squirrel pg. 149
Ictidomys mexicanus
Rock Squirrel pg. 153
Otospermophilus variegatus

Texas Antelope Squirrel pg. 141
Ammospermophilus interpres

Black-tailed Prairie Dog pg. 165
Cynomys ludovicianus

Box colors match the
corresponding section of the book.

CHECK LIST/INDEX

Use the boxes to check the mammals you've seen.

410

PHOTO CREDITS

Dr. J. Scott Altenbach: 126 (Pocketed, Long-nosed, Northern Yellow, Seminole), 127 (Southern Yellow, Bonneted)

Randall D. Babb: 125 (Ghost-faced), 126 (Western Yellow), 252 (main)

Robert Baker: 173 (Jones's)

Roger W. Barbour: 173 (Yellow-faced)

Danny Barron: 346

Troy L. Best: 71 (Chihuahuan)

Rick and Nora Bowers: 59 (Western), 64 (Cactus), 65 (White-ankled, Rock), 68 (main), 78, 82 (bottom inset), 85 (Gulf tan morph, Merriam's), 88, 91 (Yellow-nosed), 92, 94, 97 (Eastern White-throated), 107 (Mexican), 120, 122, 125 (Pipistrelle, California, Townsend's), 126 (Long-tongued, Long-legged, Western Red, Cave), 127 (Free-tailed), 150 (inset), 172 (Botta's), 184, 198, 212, 226, 228 (main), 240 (both insets), 254, 256 (all), 285, 286, 288, 302, 308 (top, middle, and right insets), 312 (bottom inset), 316 (left inset), 336 (both), 344 (top, middle, and bottom left insets), 382, 384 (both)

Joe Calomeni: 320

Guy N. Cameron: 173 (Attwater's)

Kathy Adams Clark/KAC Productions: 138

E. R. Degginger/Dembinsky Photo Associates: 46

Larry Ditto/KAC Productions: 368 (main)

Phil A. Dotson/Photo Researchers, Inc.: 232 (main)

Jerry Dragoo: 216 (main), 222, 224 (main)

Joe Fischer: 142

Richard B. Forbes, Ph.D.: 97 (Mexican), 128, 130, 140

Tony Gallucci: 224 (bottom inset)

Christine Hass: 216 (inset), 252 (bottom left inset)

John O. Hollister: 214

Gerald C. Kelley/Photo Researchers, Inc.: 232 (inset)

Gary Kramer: 368 (middle inset)

Stephen J. Krasemann/Photo Researchers, Inc.: 210

Dwight Kuhn: 71 (Plains)

Maslowski Productions: 44, 182, 193, 366, 368 (top and bottom left insets)